LEVEL UP
YOUR ESSAYS

INGER MEWBURN is the Director of Researcher Development at the Australian National University and creator of the popular blog *The Thesis Whisperer*, where she gives advice to PhD students. Inger is the author of *How to Tame Your PhD*, *How to be an Academic* and *Becoming an Academic*, and co-author with Katherine Firth and Shaun Lehmann of *How to Fix Your Academic Writing Trouble*.

KATHERINE FIRTH manages learning programs for undergraduates and graduates in university settings, and has been developing students as writers for more than a decade. She runs writing workshops for doctoral students including helping to found the Thesis Boot Camp program. Katherine currently runs the academic program at International House, a college of the University of Melbourne. She is co-author of *Your PhD Survival Guide* and gives writing advice on her blog *Research Degree Insiders*.

SHAUN LEHMANN is currently an Academic Language and Learning Facilitator at the University of New South Wales in Sydney. Previously he taught academic skills and writing at the Australian National University, lectured in anthropology and human genetics, and was a teacher of English as a second/additional language in Japan.

A NewSouth book

Published by
NewSouth Publishing
University of New South Wales Press Ltd
University of New South Wales
Sydney NSW 2052
AUSTRALIA
newsouthpublishing.com

A catalogue record for this
book is available from the
National Library of Australia

ISBN   9781742236803 (paperback)
         9781742245126 (ebook)
         9781742249643 (ePDF)

Cover design Luke Causby, Blue Cork
Internal design Josephine Pajor-Markus

LEVEL UP
YOUR ESSAYS

HOW TO GET BETTER
GRADES AT UNIVERSITY

INGER MEWBURN // KATHERINE FIRTH // SHAUN LEHMANN

NEWSOUTH

CONTENTS

How to use this book   vi

PART 1: HOW TO GET BETTER GRADES

1 WHY YOU ARE NOT (YET) GETTING GREAT GRADES   3

    1.1 Getting started   3

    1.2 What's the difference between university essays and other writing?   3

    1.3 How your essays are marked   7

    1.4 Using your lecturers' comments   8

2 WHO IS YOUR AUDIENCE?   11

    2.1 What does marking look like from the other side?   11

    2.2 What your lecturer (really) wants from you   12

    2.3 Make it easy for your lecturer to give you a good grade   14

    2.4 How to stand out from the pack   18

3 THE (NOT-SO) SECRET FORMULA FOR A GOOD ESSAY   23

    3.1 Introductions: Starting strong   24

    3.2 Body paragraphs: Filling out the middle   26

    3.3 Finishing well: The strong conclusion   31

    3.4 Writing longer and longer essays   34

    3.5 Your level-up checklist   36

4 HOW TO WRITE A CONVINCING ARGUMENT   38

    4.1 What arguments look like (and what they don't)   38

    4.2 Using truth claims   40

    4.3 Find your essay structure within the question   43

    4.4 Organise your information with LATCH   45

    4.5 Structure your writing with diagrams   45

    4.6 Use sentence skeletons to state your arguments   56

    4.7 How to 'use theory'   57

PART 2: COMMON PROBLEMS AND HOW TO FIX THEM

5 FOCUSING ON YOUR WORDS AND SENTENCES   61

    5.1 Should I use 'I'?   62

    5.2 Get your sentences straight   62

    5.3 Signposting language   65

5.4 What passive voice is (and isn't)   67

5.5 Hedging: How to say 'I don't know' and still sound like you do   68

6 WRITING IN ACADEMIC ENGLISH   **71**

6.1 Writing in English   71

6.2 Improving your academic English   74

6.3 Advice on 'Englishes' for all students   76

7 FINISHING STRONGLY WITH EDITING   **79**

7.1 Setting priorities for editing   79

7.2 How to slash words without trashing your work   80

7.3 The final stages   83

7.4 Common editing mistakes and missteps   87

7.5 How to use feedback to improve your writing   89

PART 3: PLANNING FOR NEXT TIME

8 RESEARCH AND NOTE-TAKING   **93**

8.1 Different kinds of evidence   93

8.2 How to find evidence   95

8.3 Active reading strategies   98

8.4 Active note-taking strategies   101

8.5 Taking notes that turn into writing   107

9 PLAN YOUR WAY TO (ALMOST) PERFECTION   **115**

9.1 Do you know how you actually spend your time?   115

9.2 The power of self-reflection   117

9.3 Write to find the plan   117

9.4 Focus and create a 'flow state'   120

9.5 Work while you sleep!   126

9.6 Effective 'last-minute writers'   127

AFTERWORD: DEVELOPING YOUR WRITING BEYOND ESSAYS   **129**

REFERENCE LIST   **131**

RECOMMENDED READING   **132**

ACKNOWLEDGMENTS   **133**

INDEX   **134**

HOW TO USE THIS BOOK

This is the second book on writing that the authors have done together. Our previous book, *How to Fix Your Academic Writing Trouble*, was written for PhD students and working academics. People loved that book and immediately asked us to share our ideas for people just starting at university. *Level Up Your Essays* is the result.

> How do you feel when you work hard on an essay but don't get the mark you want? You might feel dispirited, demotivated, even depressed. For your next essay you might work even harder, way harder than your classmates, and still might not see an improvement in your grades.
>
> We are here to tell you: working hard is important, but so is working *smarter.*

This book shows you how to write a better university essay: one that earns you the marks you deserve for all your hard work. This book is for anyone who needs to write essays in the arts, sciences and professional disciplines, and wants to improve their academic results.

You may feel you are doing everything 'right' in your university studies. You might be doing all the reading and spending hours on your essays, but at the end of semester find your grades are still disappointing. There are lots of reasons why someone like you might pick up a book like this, from just wanting to get an idea of what is expected from university-level essay writing, to needing to get good grades so you can go on to the postgraduate or professional pathway of your dreams. You might have already had a grade you didn't feel reflected the work you put in, or you might feel like everyone else 'just gets it' and you don't. It's never too early or too late to read this book and benefit from it!

What's more, the challenges you are facing are more common than you think.

> If you are motivated enough to pick up this book and read it, you are committed and willing to put in the work. You're already at university, so you already have the capacity to succeed.
>
> The piece of the puzzle you're missing is that university essays are different from other kinds of writing you have learned to do. Once you understand how and why they are different you will be better placed to write a great essay. In this book we will show you some tools and techniques that will help you achieve the results you want.

You might have been told you were a good writer in high school. If you have been in the workforce before starting university, you might have been praised for your neat reports and concise briefing notes. Some of you might have taken the huge step of moving away from your home country to study in Australia. Different countries teach different styles of writing; what worked at home might not work in Australia.

If you are not getting good grades in university, it's often a sign you need to move beyond a high school–style of academic writing. Unfortunately, the way you were taught to write before university does not produce the kind of essays that get a Distinction, or higher, at university. (A 'Distinction' grade is sometimes called a H2A, B+ or 2.1; it's the grade you usually need to go on to postgraduate study.)

The disconnect between high school–style essays and those you are asked to write at university is a well-known problem. So well-known, in fact, that a whole profession of experts, like ourselves, exists to help you make the transition.

We called this book *Level Up Your Essays* partly because some of us love video games and mostly because we like the sentiment. To 'level up' means that your efforts in a game have been rewarded. 'Grinding' means doing the same thing over and over, in exactly the same way; it is boring and doesn't help you make progress fast. Instead, to make faster progress, you need to do things differently. When you go up a level you get shiny stars and a different, more rewarding gaming experience. Going up a level always feels great, especially if you have worked hard for it. Levelling up in a game gives you access to new weapons, new armour and more difficult boss fights. Levelling up in your writing will give you better grades, and access to higher degrees and more job opportunities.

In this book we show you the 'hidden rules' that your university lecturers know about writing but fail to tell you. Your teachers don't hide this information deliberately; mostly they have just forgotten what it's like to be a beginner. Sometimes they give you plenty of feedback to help you improve, but the feedback may not make much sense to you. Giving practical feedback is a complex task and most of your university lecturers are content-matter experts, not writing experts. (In this book, we'll use the word 'lecturer' to mean the person who teaches you and marks your work. At your university, that person could also be called a tutor, supervisor, lab leader, advisor or teaching assistant.)

We are located in Australia, where the university system is similar to the higher education system in the UK. We are confident the advice we offer in this book will be applicable for students working in English-speaking universities in the UK, New Zealand and Australia. It will also be useful for exchange students who have come from English-speaking universities with very different norms, including those in the US, Canada and India. We have worked with students from around the world; we know there are many different 'Englishes' and many conventions around writing. There are also differences between different disciplines, and even different classes in the same degree! We'll do our best to give you good 'generic' advice, but you should check with your lecturers, or your university's writing centre, if you are not sure how the advice applies to your specific circumstances.

University writing centres – also called academic skills centres, learning hubs, or language and learning centres – provide feedback and advice on drafts of your writing. Most also offer workshops to help you develop skills like the ones we discuss in this book:

writing and structuring essays, taking good notes, and planning and editing academic writing. They may also offer English as a Second or Further Language support.

Every section in this book is designed to make sense on its own. You can read the book from start to finish or you can jump around as you like, zooming in on the parts you think you need the most.

We've designed the book so that you can pick it up and use our advice for an essay that's due in a couple of weeks. We hope you will quickly adapt your writing style to university, start to feel more confident, and pick up more marks.

In the first half of the book (**Part 1**), we explain the most significant information – what you don't know you don't know! What is an essay? How do essay questions work at university? How do you structure an essay? Who is your audience? How do you write an argument? The second half of the book (**Part 2**), which you can read when you have a bit more time on your hands, includes advice

for improving specific writing skills, organising yourself and working smarter. The final section (**Part 3**) is designed to help you think about your future as a writer, beyond your current degree.

We imagined this book as a massive video game walk-through: full of step-by-step advice on how to tackle different parts of the writing process, as well as insider strategies and trouble-shooting tips for common challenges. We also give you some behind-the-scenes insights about the expectations of your new reader: the university lecturer who is marking your essay.

This book has been printed in a large format with space to do the structured exercises we recommend. Some pages are even designed to be cut out and stuck on a wall. We imagine you will use it like a favourite game guide, writing your own notes and thoughts in the blank pages so that it becomes, over time, personalised just for you.

Let's level up!

PART 1

HOW TO GET BETTER GRADES

IF YOU ONLY READ PART OF THIS BOOK, READ THE FIRST FOUR CHAPTERS.

Getting your head around these first chapters will help you tackle the biggest reasons people get disappointing grades, and the techniques that make the biggest difference in marks.

In Part 2, we give you detailed advice for specific challenges. You might want to dip in to one or two of those areas straightaway, especially if they are things you always struggle with. But Part 2 will be more useful as you progress, and as you face more and more challenging levels of writing.

So, first: Part 1. Let us tell you the secrets about how to level up your essays by writing well-structured, well-argued essays that your marker will love.

1

WHY YOU ARE NOT (YET) GETTING GREAT GRADES

1.1 GETTING STARTED

Welcome! You have picked up a book called *Level Up Your Essays* because you want to improve your university-level writing. Let's start by getting to know you a bit better.

1.2 WHAT'S THE DIFFERENCE BETWEEN UNIVERSITY ESSAYS AND OTHER WRITING?

Many students who were high performers in high school English are shocked when they get the grade for their first university-level essay. It's not unusual at all for students who got top grades in high school to find themselves getting below-average scores in their first year of university.

Likewise, professionals returning to study who have been praised for the clarity of their writing at work can suddenly find they are near the bottom of the class at university. Self-esteem plummets!

Many international students who scored great results in their IELTS test are depressed when they find out that this score bears no resemblance to their essay grades.

What is going on here?

The good news is you have not suddenly lost 30 IQ points. The problem is you've been taught to write for a particular kind of reader and now that reader has changed. The expectations of this reader are different. University-level essays are marked by academics and measured against a different ruler. To improve your grades, you just need to learn how to produce writing a university lecturer will recognise as high quality.

High schools, workplaces and universities have different readers with different expectations. Let's spend a little bit of time thinking about the differences.

High school writing

High school essays are intended to be a fairly broad assessment of your ability to write, use language, answer a question and, to a limited extent, analyse the thoughts of others.

In high school, you might have been taught to write the 'five-paragraph essay', with formulas that tell you exactly how many points to make in each paragraph. You were rewarded for following the format, for engaging with the question and for your language use. High school teachers also like to see you use a wide vocabulary, construct complex sentences and, in some instances, demonstrate a high level of skill with descriptive language.

WORKSHEET 1 // WHY DID YOU PICK UP THIS BOOK?

In the past, people have said my writing is ...

_____

_____

_____

_____

The best feedback I ever got about my writing was ...

_____

_____

_____

_____

Right now, how I feel about my writing is ...

_____

_____

_____

_____

Things about my writing I think I need to improve are ...

_____

_____

_____

_____

WORKSHEET 2 // GET SOME EXPERT FEEDBACK

What was the feedback on your recent essays?

My lecturer said my writing was ...

_____

_____

_____

_____

✳ If you already have a few assignments, see if you can find some recurring comments or themes.

I often get feedback about ...

_____

_____

_____

_____

✳ Now take your latest essay to your writing centre and get some feedback from the advisor there. Compare it to what your lecturer said.

I got feedback from the writing centre about ...

_____

_____

_____

_____

✳ How different is the feedback you are getting from these sources to the feedback you got from your high school teachers or work colleagues?

_____

_____

_____

_____

In a university essay, *taking a side and arguing for it* is the whole point. If you write like a high school student in university, your lecturer will probably tell you that you took too long to get to the point and included too much irrelevant information.

The high school essay can be quite elegant and formal. The 'argument statement' you were told to make in the introduction describes what the rest of the essay is going to do. You were taught to keep your own logical position for the conclusion, but sometimes you were told not to declare your own view at all. You might have been taught to make an argument with the 'both sides have merit' structure: 'On the one hand … On the other hand … In conclusion, it is a balance of both.'

Workplace writing

In the workplace, you typically write to explain a situation or to help someone else take action. You may not even be writing connected prose: bosses love bullet points they can digest quickly. While you may write some longer reports, writing in a business setting tends to be short form. Executive summaries, presentations and emails rule the day.

Professional writing is concise and direct, without much referencing. Writing in the workplace usually doesn't start with questioning a theory or world view: the writer must get straight to the practical point. If you do workplace writing in an academic context, your lecturers might say you are being too certain and giving shallow treatment to your subject, or that you need more evidence.

Please bear in mind that the opposite is true when you go from university back out to the workplace. Taking academic writing out into business settings is not a good idea either. When the audience changes, so should the writing.

What is a university essay?

Academic communication is often perceived as wordy, pretentious, and purposefully riddled with waffle and unnecessarily complex ways of saying things. As a result, many students approach an essay in this way, but beware!

There are some myths about academic writing that we want to bust up-front.

Academics use dense and technical language to fit a lot of information into small word counts. Any long words or sentences are there to convey extra meaning, not to pad it out with empty word-filling. If you try to imitate 'good' writing by making lengthy sentences consisting of strings of carefully linked clauses, you won't impress your lecturer. If your word choices show you spend a lot of time with a thesaurus, you will not get extra points. This doesn't make you sound 'smart'. Lecturers don't see this writing as particularly impressive so you will continue to get mediocre grades.

Importantly, your analysis and evaluation might be different from those of your classmates or even your lecturers. At university, the top grades are awarded to 'original' or 'scholarly' work, where you have to have good ideas. Don't just describe the work of others. (We talk more about these kinds of essays in Chapter 2.) Lecturers want you to write essays because they are a good way to explore ideas where there are no black-and-white answers. This means you must take a position – but be careful not to be too certain, or to overclaim (see our section in Chapter 5 on 'hedging').

Lecturers want essays that:

1 have a *persuasive argument* based on a wide range of evidence
2 *analyse and synthesise* information from multiple sources
3 present an evaluation in *clear, concise, 'no-frills' language,* while still using all the correct technical terms.
4 only need to be *read once* to be understood.

1.3 HOW YOUR ESSAYS ARE MARKED

Lots of students have never thought about how marks are assigned. Understanding the process can give you an edge.

1 You need to make your lecturer's job easier

Think about your lecturer as a person with a very hard job. Ask yourself: how can you make it easier for your lecturer to mark *your* essay? Your lecturer may have said 'make sure you include this' or 'make sure you don't do that'. Even if you think what they are asking for isn't important, your lecturer is the one assigning the grades, so just do it.

Have a look around the class, and your lecture hall. If there are a lot of students, the chances are that your lecturer will be marking a lot of essays. What can you do to stand out from the pack?

Marking is hard work! How can you avoid making it hard for the lecturer to read your work? This is why you may have been given instructions about font, size, margins or line spacing. Follow them. Chapter 2 has some more ideas about making it easy to mark your work.

2 Ignoring the rubric is a really bad idea

Most universities now give you information about how your essay will be marked, often in a table called a 'rubric'. The rubric lays out the categories you will be marked on, commonly argument, structure, grammar, critical thinking, presentation, quality of analysis and so on. The rubric lays out the expectations for achieving each grade level. (This is officially called 'criterion-referenced' assessment.)

The rubric is there to ensure fairness in marking. If you are given a copy of the marking criteria, make sure you read it and try to follow the requirements. See Chapter 2 for much more detailed information on rubrics and how to follow them properly.

3 It's a competition

To get a top grade you can't just answer the question or get the facts right: you need to stand out in the quality of your writing and your argument.

Your work is marked against the rest of your class. This is officially called 'norm-referenced' assessment, or 'grading on the curve'. Most Australian universities do not grade to a perfect normal-distribution bell curve – there is more flexibility than that. However, most universities do have general guidelines that the top grade will represent you being in the top 10 per cent (give or take a few percentage points) of your cohort.

4 You must do something qualitatively different to break the 'grade barrier'

Each grade bracket has a set of criteria. For example, a Distinction usually requires you to have a strong argument and evidence of good critical thought. The boundaries between the grades are firm. Grading is not a sliding scale: if you are at the very top of the Distinction range, it doesn't necessarily mean that if you had included one more point you would have gone up a grade. It probably means you need to do something quite different. That is, you will need to move from having a 'strong argument' to a 'scholarly argument' if you want to get a High Distinction – we will explain more about this in Chapter 4.

Some grades have 'hurdle' requirements. So getting 49 per cent and just failing might mean that you did really well on some sections, but 'fell down' on the hurdle. Hurdles can include things like answering the question, handing your essay in on time, passing a mid-term exam and class attendance.

5 There are processes to ensure quality and consistency between markers

Most universities will select a small number of essays to be 'second marked', 'moderated' or 'cross marked' by another person. This is to check that all lecturers are marking the same way. Typically, very high marks and fail grades are always second marked. Sometimes your essay will be second marked if it's difficult for someone to clearly assign a grade. Sometimes a representative essay from each grade is second marked to ensure consistency. A random selection of essays might be graded by an external examiner, to make sure all universities are giving similar grades for similar work. Your final grade might not quite match the grades you got through the semester. Your final grade may have been second marked, or adjusted to match the curve.

6 The grade is not to reward you: it is a 'seal of approval' from your university

The purpose of grades is not to tell you if you tried hard or did good work. That's the job of the descriptive or formative feedback from the lecturer, which is usually a paragraph on the cover sheet or at the end of your essay.

The purpose of grades is to tell other parts of the university, other universities and other institutions that use university grades what your skills are and where you stand relative to other students. Grades give you further opportunities – or not. You will need high grades to get into Masters and Honours programs, medicine and law degrees, and graduate programs in government, consulting and industry.

//

It turns out marking is quite complicated, and technical! Understanding what a grade is can help demystify the process, but it can also help you see where you can focus your efforts to step up to the next grade.

1.4 USING YOUR LECTURERS' COMMENTS

Handing in the essay is not the end of the learning. Use each essay as a building block towards the next one.

Use feedback to 'feed forward' to your next essay

The written comment feedback your lecturer gave on your last assignment offers the most specific and detailed advice you can get on how to improve your writing.

Read your lecturer's feedback again before you start to write your next essay. Use it to identify your strengths and weaknesses. Keep doing more of the strengths; try to fix your weaknesses.

Talk to your lecturer if you don't understand the feedback or can't see how to carry out the advice – or if you don't agree with it. Don't focus too much on getting the lecturer to change your grade unless it's obviously unfair (see below); instead, ask how to improve your future performance.

Most lecturers have office hours, drop-in sessions or appointments, and most students never go (lecturers complain about this a lot!). It can be scary to seek your lecturer out, but most lecturers are delighted to talk to students and help them improve.

If your lecturer isn't responding to your emails, reach out to the person who convenes or coordinates the subject. Also look out for other support your university might offer, including writing centres and peer learning programs.

What if your grades are unfair?

You might experience situations where you are pretty sure your essay was unfairly graded.

Sometimes people get sick or have unavoidable external challenges that affect performance. Universities are used to receiving requests for adjustments like extra time, and have processes to ensure fairness. You usually need to follow the relevant processes first.

If you have done so, and still have reason to believe that your grade should be different, there are actions you can take.

First of all, reach out and talk to someone about how you feel. You can talk to a friend, family member or the university counselling centre. It's okay to feel hurt or angry, but it can be hard to manage the complicated requirements to apply for an extension or change in grade if you can't think clearly. As Inger's therapist says: 'Calm is control'. Seek all the emotional backing that you can so you can approach the task calmly.

As long as the essay hasn't already been second marked, and the cut-off for submission of grades has not passed, a lecturer may be able to change a grade. Don't be afraid of speaking directly to the person who marked your work in the first instance. Do this as early as possible by writing a polite email explaining the situation and seeking a meeting. At the meeting, explain why you think you deserve a better grade. We also recommend taking along a support person as a witness. It doesn't often work, but sometimes, on a second read-through, your lecturer might decide you deserve a better grade.

There are processes to escalate a complaint from the lecturer to the convenor and then to more senior academics in your institution. Think about whether you really want to do this, as chasing a grade change through the bureaucracy will take a lot of time and effort. Understand that universities are large institutions that don't always communicate well. You might find yourself explaining your situation over and over again. Be patient, and persist! Keep accurate diary notes of who you talked to, when it happened and what advice you were offered. These notes will be crucial if the complaint gets complicated.

IN SUMMARY ...

* Writing in the workplace and in high school is different from writing in university. It's likely you have some writing habits that need to change.

* Focus more on understanding argument structures and how to express yourself academically than on small tweaks of vocabulary or grammar.

* Find out more about how essays are graded at your university, and use that to deliver writing that meets the requirements.

* It is essential to reflect on your writing and seek feedback from others. Use criticism to develop your weaknesses and to grow your strengths.

2

WHO IS YOUR AUDIENCE?

Your essay will be read by one very important reader: your university lecturer. This lecturer will decide if your essay answers the question, provides strong evidence, has a clear argument and is formatted correctly. This person will decide your grade.

Fortunately, you often already know your lecturer. You have met them in class and listened to their views and ideas in lectures. They may have written your subject handbook, posted advice on the online learning management system (LMS), sent out emails or provided worksheets. To write a good essay, you need to put yourself in their shoes.

If you haven't ever taught at a university, it can be hard to imagine what your essay looks like to a marker. Luckily you have us! Shaun and Katherine have marked hundreds of undergraduate essays across multiple universities on three continents, and Inger has read a lot of dissertations, which are longer versions of the same thing. Here's our insider's view of what it's like to read a student essay.

2.1 WHAT DOES MARKING LOOK LIKE FROM THE OTHER SIDE?

Okay, so your lecturer is sitting down to mark your essay. What is it like? Marking essays is a bit stressful. Lecturers know that grades matter to you, and they want to be fair, give helpful advice and help you develop your passion for their subject. They have to keep an eye out for potential collusion (where you get too much help for your essay from friends, family or tutors) or plagiarism (where you use the words and ideas of other people without acknowledging where you got them from).

Your essay will be in a large pile of other essays: maybe as many as 50 to 150. You feel like your essay is special and unique; lecturers will see it as similar to many, many others. Being different can be good, but only if you are different in the right way (as we explain later in this chapter).

Your lecturer will aim to read your essay once – you really don't want them reading it twice because that's usually a sign the first read-through didn't go well. If you wrote your essay carefully, you will have spent hours working on it and read it many times, but it should only take minutes to read. Typically, lecturers will be taking about 15–30 or so minutes to read a short essay, write feedback and decide your grade. Universities regulate how long it should take to mark an essay and often are paying for it by the hour. Many universities have rules about getting feedback to you in a short period too.

Don't count on any relationship you may have built with the lecturer to affect your grade, either positively or negatively. This marker might not even have met you, or you might be one of hundreds of students in their classes. Many essays are marked 'blind', where the lecturer only sees your student number.

2.2 WHAT YOUR LECTURER (REALLY) WANTS FROM YOU

Your lecturer and your university want you to succeed. Your lecturers are passionate about their subject, and they want to share their understanding with others: that's why they became researchers and lecturers in the first place.

The lecturer will explain what you need to do in the syllabus or handbook, in class or via email. Make sure you read these sources. They are goldmines of direct advice, exactly relevant for this class and this assignment.

Every essay will also have some basic and shared expectations. Knowing what they are can help you to try to meet them. So what do your markers want from you?

1 They want you to answer the question

Every essay starts with an essay question or prompt. You will either be given a list of questions to choose from, or be expected to craft your own question.

Essay questions come in an infinite variety of formats. We've seen essay questions phrased as questions. We've seen essay questions with multiple sub-questions. Question words like 'why', 'how', 'to what extent' and 'how important' are the easiest to spot as questions. But we've also seen implied questions: for example, when the prompt is just a quote, with the instruction 'Discuss'.

Essay questions can be deliberately vague, leaving room for interpretation. Mostly, lecturers assign essay questions that do not have a straightforward answer, or that offer multiple possible answers. You have to intuit

Whatever your essay question looks like, there are three parts to an essay question. (You can also use these to craft your own question.)

1 *A topic.* This is what your essay is about.
2 *A way to limit the topic.* This might be a phrase like 'to what extent', a range of dates, a theory, a name and so on.
3 *An implied argument.* It's not always easy to spot, but every essay question has an implied argument, which you may or may not agree with.

these answers and decide whether they are true, partially true or false. Then you argue your position on the answer. Your marker wants to see what argument you will make and how you make it.

However, even vague-sounding questions are not an invitation to 'go off topic'.

Take a few minutes to talk to your lecturer about your understanding of the essay topic before you fully commit to writing. Check that your proposed piece of work lines up with what is expected. Ask the lecturer if your understanding of the question is correct, and then briefly describe what you'd like to do to answer that question.

The lecturer might save you from making major errors, they might give you reassurance you are on the right track, or they might give you an insider's tip to help you level up even more.

It's common for students to wander off into another issue, idea or personal passion rather than sticking to the problem they've been asked to write about. Don't be one of those students!

2 They want you to take a position and argue for it (even if they don't agree with you)

Essay questions usually involve verbs like 'describe', 'discuss', 'examine' and 'analyse'. While it might seem that terms like 'discuss' and 'explore' aren't asking for an argument, trust us: they are. (For more on writing a convincing argument, see Chapter 4.)

> Never assume that an essay 'discussion' is about, you know, actually discussing things. At university, you must *always* write to persuade the reader, not just share what you have found out. No matter which verb the question uses, they should all be treated as meaning 'make a convincing argument'.

In high school, you might have encountered teachers who wanted you to parrot back their own opinions in response to essay questions. You may also have been taught to take a 'balanced' approach, where you avoid taking one side. This is rare at universities. Almost all lecturers are asking you to explore a topic with your own research. Most lecturers will give good marks to essays that disagree with their own stated position – if you argue it well enough.

3 They are more interested in **how** you argue than the position you take

The main purpose of a university essay is to put forward an argument. This doesn't mean we want you to have a fight!

In everyday life, arguing with a family member or friend involves emotions. You might shout or stamp your foot. In an academic argument, we don't want lots of aggression and emotion. We like to keep things nice.

> An academic argument is 'a connected series of statements or reasons intended to establish a position (and, hence, to refute the opposite); a process of reasoning' – according to the *Oxford English Dictionary*.

The difference between a fight and an academic argument is that you use reasons to defend your point of view, and those reasons should be based on good evidence. Katherine likes to use the analogy of a courtroom: you are a lawyer using evidence to make a case to a judge.

There are two main ways to ensure the reasons you use to support your argument can be defended:

1 Generate data or highlight relevant facts sourced from your academic reading on the subject to support your case.
2 Use someone else's argument, preferably one by an academic or other credible expert, to support your case.

Not all kinds of evidence are equal. We will talk more about what kind of evidence academics will accept in Chapter 8.

4 They want you to clearly state your argument at the start, not reveal it at the end

An introduction for academic writing is a summary of your argument. You should have your argument, and the answer to the question, stated in the first paragraph or so. Don't be afraid to just say it straight – 'This essay argues that …' – followed by one or two sentences to explain your point. That way the reader can gauge whether the rest of your essay is in line with your stated position.

> Don't keep your argument a secret! As Inger's PhD supervisor used to say: 'Academic writing is not a murder mystery: we want to know who is guilty in the first paragraph.'

If the marker reaches the end of the introduction and still doesn't have a clear understanding of your position, they will have to guess. And they might guess wrong. If you save the argument for the conclusion, the marker needs to read your essay twice, which cuts down on the time they have left to write careful feedback. If it's hard to work out what you are arguing, your work might be perceived as 'poorly argued', 'not well thought out', or maybe even 'meandering' or 'wandering'.

We talk more about introductions in Chapter 3 and how to frame arguments in Chapter 4.

5 They want you to argue the main point all the way through your essay

A research essay is most effective when you identify the most important point, and stick with it in every single paragraph. You might be tempted to try to cram in lots of different important points, but this means your essay will be a shallow, unfocused list. Sticking with a single point means you get a chance to go deeper and engage with more detailed evidence. This is another reason why the 'five-paragraph essay' structure (introduction, point one, point two, counterpoint, conclusion) can give you problems at university. You are only using one section of your essay to argue for the strongest point, then you waste time on an additional, different point and then on the opposing argument.

Instead, work out the strongest argument you can think of and argue that, using however many paragraphs it takes within the word count. We explain how to plan with paragraphs in Chapter 3.

2.3 MAKE IT EASY FOR YOUR LECTURER TO GIVE YOU A GOOD GRADE

Make your essay easy to mark and you will get better grades.

> Many students are surprised to hear that essays that achieve the highest grades are often the easiest ones to read. That's right – the best essays are often straightforward. They are written in clear language with a clear response to the question and a position on the topic.

A really bad essay is also easy to mark. If you don't answer the question, copy and paste long quotes without attribution, forget to have an argument or leave out important sections, it's clear that you won't be getting a good grade, even if you put in a lot of effort or felt passionate about the subject.

An essay that is hard to grade is usually a borderline case. In one of these essays you may have written some great parts but then wandered off topic for a whole paragraph. Or you slightly misunderstood the question, and so your answer was slightly off topic the whole way through. Or you wrote in a confusing way, using imprecise language and not clearly stating your argument. In short: your marker had to guess what you meant. It's hard to decide if you deserve a great mark or a mediocre one, so they split the difference. Lots and lots of essays end up getting Credits rather than Distinctions for this reason.

Some lecturers will give you the benefit of the doubt, but strict rubrics and cross marking usually reduces the chance your lecturer will go soft on you. You need to make it easy for your lecturer to see that you have met the grade.

How to make your essay easy for your lecturer to mark

Here are the main things you need to do.

1 Write clearly

If you don't write clearly, the marker will have to read the sentence, paragraph, phrase or section again … and maybe again. If it's still not clear, the marker will have to guess, or will skip it and move on.

Unclear writing has problems at the sentence or paragraph level that are not necessarily about 'correct' grammar. Language that's ambiguous and vague can be confusing. Using prepositions like 'this' over and over again, especially at the start of sentences, forces your reader to constantly backtrack and reread the text to work out what you are saying. Write this way and you are likely to be told you write in a way that is 'waffly', 'unclear' or 'woolly'.

It's very easy to improve the clarity of your writing. Make sure you have a break between writing your essay and submitting it. Reading it over one more time before handing it in will help you catch places where there's a gap between what you meant to say and what's actually on the page.

Longer term, work on improving your editing skills. Being able to rewrite or restructure your work to be clearer is a superpower, and we talk more about that in Chapters 5 and 7. There are lots of great books on writing well; check out our recommended reading list at the end of the book.

2 Break things up into easy-to-read chunks

Overly long sentences, paragraphs or sections with too many ideas crammed in are really hard to disentangle. So, break them down. You can use headings or topic sentences at the beginning of paragraphs to show what each chunk of writing is doing. Opinions vary widely on which way is 'right', so check in with your lecturer before you start writing.

If feedback on your writing suggests your sentences are the problem, the easiest fix is to make sure that each sentence only contains one idea. If a given idea is finished, put in a full stop. A nice rule of thumb to use is to check the sentence length. If it's more than 40 words long, it probably has more than one idea and you need to split it up.

Paragraphs are often structured to have a topic sentence, one piece of evidence and an explanation of that evidence … and that's it. We'll talk more about paragraphs in Chapter 3.

3 Tidy it up before you hand it in

Lots of little errors make your writing look sloppy or rushed. While grammar, spelling, formatting and citation style are usually a minor part of your grade, they are still important. Some rubrics will take up to 10 per cent off for these kinds of small mistakes. (We have advice on things like apostrophes and dashes in Chapter 7.)

With today's technology, it has never been easier to provide tidy work. Use your computer's spellcheck and online tools like Grammarly. Use the citation managers in your writing software, or the specialised ones that are provided by your university.

Making your text all the same size, colour and font literally takes seconds. This means your marker doesn't get distracted by any mess, and they don't have to spend time giving you feedback on it. Most universities have services that give you free feedback on your writing, but they won't usually check this stuff for you.

4 Pay attention to the small requests

Most lecturers will have a list of seemingly small requests associated with an essay assessment. Commonly, these include a cover sheet, certain fonts and spacing, a minimum number of references, and a particular citation style.

These requests are usually there for a reason. For example, making sure your text conforms to any rules you have been given about double spacing or margins will make it easier for your marker to write feedback on your essay.

Pay attention to these small requests: it's good practice for later on in your work life anyway.

5 Pay special attention to the marking rubric

Universities make lecturers use rubrics to ensure grading is transparent and fair. Most courses will include the rubric in the class guide, handbook or syllabus. Usually the rubric will test the 'learning outcomes' listed in your syllabus.

If you can't find the rubric, ask your lecturer. The same information might be called 'marking criteria', 'marking guide', 'grading scheme' or 'learning outcomes' instead. A few lecturers don't use rubrics, but they will usually have a reason why! If your lecturer doesn't use a rubric, ask them how they know an essay is worth a High Distinction and listen carefully to what they say. Did they mention the quality of the writing or the amount of evidence? Did they say anything about presentation? Listen for things they like and dislike.

> Don't be afraid to ask your lecturer questions about how your work is marked. Better still, ask them to share an example of a good essay from a previous year with you.

A well-written rubric sets out how many marks you can gain for different parts of the assessment. We call this 'weighting'. You will get marks for argument and research, but also for correct citation and good writing (these are the 'marking criteria'). For example, if you notice that your lecturer gives quite a lot of weight to research, you might want to take the time to add more references to your work to

Table 1: Typical marking rubric

Criteria	Marks available	Level of achievement				
		Does not meet expectations	Minimum standard	Almost meets expectations	Meets expectations	Exceeds expectations
Effectively uses information resources and evidence	30%	Fails to meet the minimum standard.	Gathers a minimum number of resources from class materials.	Relies on class materials and a small number of independently researched sources, which are accurately described.	Shows wide and relevant independent resource-gathering skills, which are critically analysed.	Shows wide and relevant independent resource-gathering skills, which are critically analysed. May show creativity or resourcefulness in finding sources or in creating original data.
Effectively synthesises and organises information	30%	Fails to meet the minimum standard.	Collects information and places the evidence in a logical order.	Organises information according to an argument, synthesising and ordering information concisely.	Develops a clearly stated argument by synthesising and analysing evidence to support academic claims.	Develops a clearly stated and original argument by synthesising and analysing evidence to contribute a creative or unique insight.
Depth and breadth of understanding	30%	Fails to meet the minimum standard.	Demonstrates misunderstandings about basic concepts and does not connect in-class material with a wider context.	Demonstrates understanding of concepts and successfully connects material with a wider context.	Uses theoretical, methodological or ethical understanding to explain concepts and successfully connect material with a wider context.	Uses theoretical, methodological or ethical understanding to develop new concepts or connect material with a wider context in creative ways.
Conventions, writing and presentation	10%	Fails to meet the minimum standard.	Rarely uses proper sentence structure, grammar, punctuation, citation style or spelling.	Uses proper sentence structure, grammar, punctuation, citation style and spelling.	Writes fluent and engaging text, using communication skills to engage or persuade the reader. Few errors.	Writes elegant, compelling text using communication skills to engage and persuade the reader. No errors.

demonstrate you have read widely. If you do this, don't just add in lots of extra stuff – make sure it's relevant material and you have actually taken the time to read the articles you cite. Be very careful about what counts as a source – for more on this issue, consult Chapter 8 (Section 8.1).

You will find lecturers offer additional explanations of their expectations for essay writing during lectures and tutorials, and in your online LMS. Listen carefully and write down these tips!

The rubric is a useful diagnostic tool so don't throw it away at the end of the semester. Take the rubric, the essay and the feedback you received to your learning centre or writing centre to get help on where you could do better next time.

A marking rubric example

A rubric is one way to present a marking guide or grading scheme. Set out in a visual format, the rubric tells you which aspects of your essay will gain points, and what percentage of the overall grade is impacted by your spelling vs your argument vs your research. You may be surprised.

The most common rubric format is a grid. The criteria – what you are judged on – are listed down the left-hand side. The number of marks available for any aspect of the essay, sometimes called a 'weighting', is also listed. Then the level of achievement for each criteria is listed, usually running from lowest level of attainment to highest level of attainment. The levels will often match your overall grade (e.g. a top grade will be given for work that consistently 'Exceeds Expectations', and a passing grade will be given for work that meets the minimum standard).

See page 17 for a typical example rubric. Then grab one of your old essays and try

grading yourself against this rubric to get a sense of what it's like to assess your own work.

2.4 HOW TO STAND OUT FROM THE PACK

Throughout this book we give you the solid writing advice that will take your essays up a grade or two. (Feel free to skip forward to Chapter 3 for now if that's what you're looking for.) But if you are regularly getting that Distinction grade, you might want to take on the big boss: the A grade, or High Distinction. In this section we want to share some techniques that actually might take you into the stratosphere. If we read an essay like this, we wouldn't just be impressed – we'd tell our colleagues about it.

You should know that some of the recommendations in this section are high risk. People who get unbelievably high marks in one class using these techniques might only scrape into Credits in another class. These are not safe suggestions. (Everything else we write in the book is pretty safe though!)

Understand your context, audience and discipline

If your lecturer is more of a stickler for correct form and style, maybe hand in a less experimental essay that conforms to the structures we give you elsewhere in the book.

Your audience is your lecturer, and a good way to find out what your lecturer wants is to go up to them after a class or in their office hours and talk to them! You can ask if your planned approach is a good idea in general terms, and then listen to how they respond. If they are negative about your idea, then that gives you a lot of useful information. You might also ask for an

At the really top level you need to be more sophisticated about your *context, audience* and *discipline.*
- Understanding your *context* means being able to 'read the room' and gather clues about what kinds of behaviour are rewarded. For example:
- If your lecturer encourages you to be critical and challenging in class, or the readings are highly theoretical, then that is a clue that such approaches are likely to be welcome in your essays.

example of a strong essay from a previous year, especially if the subject is new to you. Shaun did this when he moved from science to social science, and it was really helpful. Find out what your marker thinks is good writing and write that way.

Finally, understanding your discipline means knowing the difference between what makes a strong argument in different subjects. For instance, in a discipline like psychology, you want to go with the mainstream scholarship: there are well-established answers about what causes depression, or how to treat trauma, for example. If you are going to disagree, be very sure you are right and have evidence to back up your case. Think about why your lecturer might have strong opinions. In some cases, such as in psychology, making assumptions and getting the answer wrong means cruel and dangerous treatment of human beings.

Other disciplines are far more flexible about what 'truth' means; as Katherine often told her students, 'There are no right answers in English literature; there are lots of good

answers, and a few wrong answers.' As long as you avoid the wrong answers (e.g. don't say the novel *Jane Eyre* (1847) is 'a modern play', or that there is any justification for the racism in *Othello*), you'll be fine taking an unusual approach.

Avoid 'boring'

When you are working on your essay, it's the only essay in the world to you. If you care about your studies, then you are interested in the material. Also, if you are a newcomer to university, you are probably working on this material for the first time. It's all exciting and noteworthy to you.

However, if your essay has covered the content from class, used the recommended readings, met the requirements of the rubric and nothing more, it's probably not going to be 'original', or any of the other words that markers use to describe the top essays, like 'compelling', 'provocative', or having a 'unique approach'.

To move from a very good essay that ticks all the boxes into a *scholarly and original essay* that gets the top marks is tough. You need to stand out from the pack, and not look like everyone else.

An essay that looks like everyone else's is 'boring'. Boring is good if you aren't yet getting Distinctions, but if you have been stuck in Distinction-land forever and are ready to move up, then it's time to avoid boring. Here are some ways to do that.

1   Have an unusual argument

It doesn't have to be extreme, but if everyone in your class is going to write about how *Romeo and Juliet* is a tragic story about 'star-crossed lovers', maybe write an essay about how Mercutio is the real victim of the warring families.

2   Pick the 'unpopular' question or topic

If you are given a list of possible questions, pick the one you think will be unusual or challenging: this gives you a good chance of standing out. The 'easy' question everyone else is planning to do probably isn't easy either, but deliberately choosing the unpopular, challenging one sends a signal to your lecturer that you want to aim high. If you're not sure which question will be unpopular, casually ask a few classmates what they have planned and then bravely head out in a different direction!

3   Use a theory

Many students read about theories, they learn about theories, they see books and articles using theories, but they don't actually start using a theory themselves. So, pick a theory and try to use it in your next essay as a lens through which to look at your topic. You don't have to be totally convinced by the theory before you start – essays can be a good way to explore which theory is right for you. (See more about using theory in Chapter 4).

4   Get way more focused

If you look at journal articles or doctoral theses, you will see they are amazingly specific. Katherine wrote her thesis of 100 000 words on poets and composers collaborating on art song in London between 1935 and 1950.

Inger filmed about ten students for her thesis about architecture students' use of gesture in design studio classes. Both these projects are examples of what we mean by 'niche'. Niche is exactly what we are looking for in academic research, so if you want to write essays that show you have potential to go on to postgraduate study this is a good place to start. How specific do you think you can get? If you are worried you are getting too narrow, go chat to your lecturer during their office hours.

5   Go beyond the reading list

Bring in readings from other subjects you are taking. Bring in research in other languages. Talk to a librarian and see if you can access unusual resources like rare books or archives. These can give you a unique edge.

6   Disagree (in a polite, academic way) with your readings

If you review the research and come to a conclusion that is different from the conclusion in your readings – or even different to your lecturer's conclusions – you can say so in a professional and courteous way. You'll have seen this happen quite a bit in your readings. Academics love to disagree with each other in their articles so have a go yourself. Be careful: you'll need evidence for your position, remember? If you are nervous about starting down this track, make sure you have some other books or articles to back you up.

7   Start to build a 'professional identity position' in your essay

This advice is particularly for people studying in areas that have a profession attached: social worker, psychologist, teacher, etc. Try to write essays as if you were already working in that space. Look to published work by professionals to get an idea of how this is done – or make friends with the mature age students in your class. One of the reasons mature age students tend to get better grades is they already have a professional identity and experience that they are bringing into their essays.

What *not* to do when you are trying to stand out

We have all seen people use these super high-risk strategies only to crash and burn. You may also know someone who seems to be successfully using these strategies, but if they suggest you do the same, listen courteously and ignore their advice!

1 Don't include humour in an essay

Jokes are often not nearly as funny as you think they are, and lots of jokes rely on cruelty or inappropriateness for their punchlines, which is not a good idea in an academic setting. What's more, academic humour is … not really humour, actually. What academics really find funny is an ironic placement of a semicolon … which might not be what you think of when you hear the word 'humour'.

2 Don't disagree with the lecturer/ readings on the basis of life experience

Your personal experience is valid, but usually doesn't produce the right kind of evidence for a research essay unless you view it through a theoretical lens. Some of our most brilliant students are creating an individual theoretical

approach through their personal experience, but it's very hard and they will be facing quite a lot of opposition. It's much safer to do it through already published theory and evidence.

3 Don't do anything involving a cutesy form

You will all have seen the viral essay that rhymed, or the one where the first letter in each line spelled 'NEVER GONNA GIVE YOU UP'. Please do not do this. Your marker might smile when they first realise the trick form but they will soon get bored with it. It's very hard to write a longer piece in a very strict form, so you are just creating extra work for you and the lecturer, and they still won't give you a good grade.

4 Don't try to surprise the marker

Avoid anything that will be shocking, surprising or mysterious. The point of an undergraduate essay is to show you understand the content and are able to construct a coherent argument, with a clear introduction, that answers the question. It's enough of a surprise if you do this well.

Mostly, what will make you stand out from the pack is writing an essay that:

- has a well-focused topic
- offers a strong argument
- demonstrates deep research
- answers the question, and
- shows that you are starting to develop your own voice and position.

To stand out even more, take each of those points and push it a bit further:

Well-focused topic	➲	Super-focused topic
Strong argument	➲	Scholarly argument
Deep research	➲	Original research
Starting to develop your own position	➲	Confidently stating your own professional voice and position

If we could give generic advice on how to stand out … you wouldn't stand out. It is up to you to work out your own unique, original and scholarly way of thinking, and show that thinking through your essays.

IN SUMMARY …

* Understanding your audience – your lecturer – helps you to communicate effectively with them.

* Your lecturer wants you to answer the question and have a clear argument.

* Think about being original, but not *too* original.

* Start talking to your lecturers! Use them to help you interpret the rubric, get feedback on a past assignment or check you are on the right track for an upcoming essay.

3

THE (NOT-SO) SECRET FORMULA FOR A GOOD ESSAY

An essay has four main components:

1 **An introduction.** Where you state the argument you are going to make in the context of the broader problem you have been given to explore. You should give the answer to the question here and outline the argument you intend to make.

2 **The body of the essay.** Where you lay out all the evidence and reasons to support your argument. Each paragraph should be purposeful and include a sentence that links back to your main argument in some way.

3 **A conclusion.** Strong writing has a circular structure: your conclusion should relate directly to your introduction, reminding us why your answer was convincing, based on your body paragraphs.

4 **A reference list.** A list of the sources of evidence you have used to prove your argument, or to put your argument in context.

Michel de Montaigne in the sixteenth century was the first person to write his thoughts down on a particular subject and call it an 'essay'. Over time, the form has evolved into a standard piece of academic assessment that is used by university lecturers to test their students' critical thinking and communication skills.

The classic advice on writing an essay is: 'Say what you're going to say; say it; then say what you've said.' It's helpful advice for staying on track, and for understanding why essays are structured the way they are.

All four main parts of an essay are important for getting a good grade. Each part has specific expectations about what it should look like, what is in it, and how it is related to the other parts.

Your lecturer usually wants to see these parts in that order. Don't muck about with the basic essay form in an attempt to be clever – unless you are clearly instructed to do so in the rubric!

Let's start at the beginning: the introduction.

3.1   INTRODUCTIONS: STARTING STRONG

A good introduction sets the standard for a good essay. By the end of the first paragraph, the reader will often have a sense of what grade you will get, because you will have already shown you have answered the question with a strong argument and compelling evidence.

However, if you have a poor opening, your marker will have to attend more closely to your text. They will have to read more carefully to try to work out your argument, structure and position. If you only *imply* your answer to the question instead of stating it clearly, your marker might miss it. They might spot all the other weaknesses in your essay though.

Don't write essays that are basically a continuous introduction, where the problem is stated over and over again in different ways. This is not an essay. A list of facts or opinions loosely joined together is not an essay either, so your introduction shouldn't look like a list.

High school essays, newspaper articles, blog posts and non-fiction books use a number of writing tricks to 'hook' you into reading further. For example, they may start with a quote, a definition or a surprising backstory. But academics read to be informed; they are looking for information. In Australia, they usually won't give your research essay 'hook' many marks.

Some hooks will actually disadvantage your grade. Overreaching a claim to relevance, for example, means you tip into exaggeration. Starters like 'since the beginning of time' or 'everyone in the world' are red flags to a marker. They start thinking, 'Actually, is that true for all times? For every single person? Probably not.' Don't start an academic off thinking this way – it goes nowhere good for you!

The secret formula for a great introduction

There is a formula for a strong introduction paragraph, three key 'moves' your marker is expecting you to make. *The Craft of Research*, the 'go-to' text for beginning researchers, summarises these moves as follows:

1   Give the relevant background to the problem.
2   State the problem.
3   Give your response to the problem.

'Relevant background' doesn't mean a long explanation of everything that has happened up until now: it's a 'sound bite' that orients the reader to the general topic being discussed. (If you need to give more background, see the next section on context paragraphs). This move should be quickly followed by a summary of the specific part of the problem you want to address and then your response to the problem. Your response to the problem is basically a statement of your argument, in miniature.

It's sometimes hard to imagine what these instructions would look like in practice, so we have some totally made-up examples from social science and science. Here's the question:

How should the trade of unicorn hair remedies for plantar fasciitis be regulated so we better preserve this resource for future generations?

From economics/political science:

(Background to the problem) The global market for unicorn hair has been growing in recent decades, leading to shortages in exporting countries. Growth in exports has not been matched by growth in unicorn numbers, leading to massive price rises in countries that supply the global market, such as Australia. **(Statement of the problem – what is happening now)** The price of unicorn hair has tripled in Australia, putting this ingredient, commonly used in traditional medicine, out of the reach of many working-class people. People who cannot access their traditional remedies legally have been blockading farms and export depots, putting the entire unicorn hair industry at risk. **(Response to the problem/statement of the argument)** This essay will argue that raising the tariffs on unicorn hair is the most effective way to combat this unrest in Australia. Finding appropriate ways to regulate the market in unicorn hair is critically important for social cohesion in Australia and tariffs are the most efficient means to achieve the outcome.

Note that we have included the 'this essay will argue that' sentence form, to make sure the reader knows exactly what the argument is from the very beginning. You might then go on to list what is coming up in the essay and in what order.

In a science essay, you would have the same 'moves' in your introduction, but you might execute them in a slightly different style. The question might imply how to do those moves differently.

How does unicorn hair act as a remedy for plantar fasciitis, and what are the challenges of researching this traditional medicine?

(Background to the problem) Unicorn hair is used as a traditional remedy for plantar fasciitis. Scientists have been working since the 1980s to determine why it is effective in the treatment of this common foot injury (Wahid-Alqarn and Inikoni, 2016). **(Statement of the problem – what is happening now)** Scientists have explored the structure of Australian and Chilean unicorn hair to try to ascertain why it can mitigate plantar fasciitis symptoms, but to date results have been inconclusive (Alailoye *et al.*, 1983; Jantuvunu et al., 2019). **(Response to the problem/statement of the argument)** This essay argues that we need more novel approaches to the study of unicorn hair structure, specifically experiments that are designed to account for regional differences.

The context paragraph

To write a focused argument, you might need to leave out material and information you gathered in your research phase. Good writers don't try to cram everything in; they are confident enough to leave some of the background material out, especially if it's beyond the scope of the essay. However, knowing what to keep and leave out is a real challenge. You will still need to show that you are aware of the wider debates, of the bigger picture.

Some of you may have been taught to write a 'funnel' introduction: one that moves from the background to the focus of the essay. In this type of introduction, you start at a global level, and then get narrower and narrower. Then you write the essay. This technique might sound like it encourages you to write the kind of overblown 'hook' we discussed earlier in the chapter, like 'since the beginning of time'. It's also hard to shift from the global to the specific in two or three sentences within your introduction, when you also need to explain your argument, set out your position and summarise the body paragraphs.

A typical, not very successful, 'funnel' introduction often looks something like this:

> Since the beginning of time, mankind has needed heroes. Some of those heroes died and became Viking ghosts. Viking ghosts cause delays to production pipelines due to decomposition of seaside materials (Corsario, 2019a), and loss of income through days lost to staff illness (Haidau, 2018). In 2016, issues with Viking ghost damage caused US$60 million to be wiped off the value of the Nikkei Index in Japan, after a particularly bad season (Omu, 2017).

Notice how there is no room for the all-important argument, and the transitions are pretty clunky.

> An alternative is to give yourself a paragraph after the introduction to explain the 'context'. This is where you include the historic backstory, explain a method or theory, show off your wider reading or deal with common misconceptions.

Here is an example of a context paragraph that explains a backstory:

> Viking ghosts are well known as a global issue for companies around the globe (Pirata, 2017). Viking ghosts cause delays to production pipelines due to decomposition of seaside materials (Corsario, 2019a), and loss of income through days lost to staff illness (Haidau, 2018). In 2016, issues with Viking ghost

damage caused US$60 million to be wiped off the value of the Nikkei Index in Japan, after a particularly bad season (Omu, 2017). Until the eighteenth century, Viking ghosts were mostly an issue for Europe and North America (Egyszarvú, 2012). One of the major ways to deal with them was unicorn hair (Pegleg, 1987; Ban, 2015). Since global trade between Europe, and the Far East and South America developed due to colonialism, Viking ghosts have come to the Pacific and South China Sea areas attached to rigging of ships, in particular in the years before the introduction of Bermuda rigging which was a less hospitable environment for ghosts in transport (Pegleg, 1987).

An introduction-plus-context-paragraph structure is easier to write, and to read, than a 'funnel' introduction. You also don't have to keep interrupting your body paragraphs to give background, and you can write a more focused middle.

//

Writing introductions is not easy. Worksheet 3 provides an exercise to help you craft your introductory paragraphs.

3.2   BODY PARAGRAPHS: FILLING OUT THE MIDDLE

The body of the essay should step your reader through the reasons and evidence that support your argument in a clear and logical order.

Unless stated in the rubric, there are no rules about how many paragraphs go in an essay. The number of paragraphs is less important than the way your paragraphs build together to help a reader follow your argument.

WORKSHEET 3 // SENTENCE SKELETONS FOR INTRODUCTIONS

Here is a helpful introduction sentence skeleton
for you to practise putting the moves into action.

This essay focuses on _____

_____

and asks / considers / explores

how / why / whether _____

_____

It has been suggested **(references)** that _____

_____

I / this essay will show / suggest / argue that _____

_____

(whatever you think in relation to that suggested idea).

I / it will look at / draw on _____
(whatever sources).

or

First I / it will _____

_____

and then _____

_____

(signpost what you'll discuss in what order).

> We encourage you to think of each paragraph as a 'chunk of thinking' – a step in the logical development of your argument.

But you also want a paragraph to be easy to read. And there are conventions about paragraph length and structure. Your paragraphs can be too long, too short or confusingly organised, which means your 'chunk of thinking' doesn't build towards a very good essay.

1 Short enough to be easy to read and keep the whole thing in mind

It's likely there are multiple steps in your argument, and multiple things to cite, explain, consider, assess and describe. If you do all of that in a long page, without breaking it up, it's easy for the reader to get lost or confused or overwhelmed. The paragraph is a way to break your writing up into smaller 'chunks' of meaning.

> Different disciplines have different styles for how long a paragraph should be, but usually a paragraph should be between one-third and one-half of a page (this will come to about 250–400 words). If it's longer than that, the marker will have trouble seeing the whole paragraph, or remembering the beginning of the paragraph by the end.

A sentence is both a written and grammatical segment, and it is roughly the length of a breath if read aloud. Similarly, a paragraph is both a writing and argument chunk, and is roughly the length of what someone can read without glancing up.

2 Long enough to explain the point you are trying to make

Academic paragraphs are rarely a single sentence long, unlike those in newspaper articles, emails and some reports. Usually you would expect somewhere between three and ten sentences in a paragraph. If your paragraphs are regularly less than 3–5 sentences long, you may get the comment from your marker that it is a 'fragment' or that 'this is not a paragraph'.

3 Structured in a way that makes it easy to read

Shorthand 'formulas' of how to write paragraphs like TEEL (Topic, Evidence, Explanation, Link) or PIE (Point, Illustration, Explanation) are good but can be a bit restrictive. Different paragraphs are doing different things. Instead, think of these acronyms as giving you a clue about the 'moves' you should be making.

Academic paragraphs should include the following 'moves': you can think about it like a 'paragraph dance'. If your marker doesn't see these moves, you are not dancing – you are just jumping about.

1 **Write a topic 'sentence'**: This is a summary of the content of the paragraph. A topic 'sentence' might be a phrase (part of a sentence), or two sentences. Generally, the topic sentence should be at the beginning of the paragraph, but sometimes it's more appropriate to make it the conclusion of the paragraph. Wherever it appears, you will need one.

2 **Explain the step in the argument you are making, in your own words**: Even if you are presenting other people's evidence, using your own words shows the marker you have understood the evidence.

3 **Give evidence that shows your point isn't just your opinion**: Even reflective pieces and opinion pieces should have evidence. But for research essays, demonstrating the depth and sophistication of the scholarly evidence you have found, analysed and synthesised is critical. You might use numbers, dates and/or citations of other scholars who have discussed the topic; you might also use quotes, tables, figures or other data.

4 **Use or explain this evidence**: Now you have stated the evidence, you need to put it into action. You may also need to define terms, or compare your evidence with other data. This is the place to synthesise the evidence, bringing it together with other evidence. This is also the place to explain how the evidence is impacted by analysis, theory or context. This is sometimes called 'interpretation' or 'explanation'.

5 **Signal what is coming next**: You don't always need a specific sentence if the progression is obvious, but a link-forward sentence is never wasted if it makes sure no one gets lost in the paragraph break.

For example, in a history essay you might use these moves like this:

(Two topic sentences: one signalling the shift from the previous paragraph, and one summarising the contents of this paragraph) On the other hand, cheaper alternative methods were also available to achieve these practical outcomes. In Dubloon's time, it was known that using water from a clean spring 'withouten taint' (p. 55) avoided the chance of ghost germs, and adding salt or consecrated wine was also effective at removing ghosts. **(Explain this step of the argument in your own words; give evidence using dates, names, places and references)** Dubloon used all of these options during the Napoleonic Wars (1803–15) when unicorn hair was harder to access, as the main centres of the unicorn industry were in the Austro-Hungarian Empire and Albania (see Egyszarvú, 2012; Njëbrirësh, 1991). **(Use the evidence, comparing it to other data)** By the 1780s, when Polly was using unicorn hair, other options were also available for laying Viking ghosts in the rigging. Using rum and lime cordial applied when the moon was full was common (Pegleg, 1987). Additionally, the new style of Bermuda rigging was replacing the older style of square rigging through the nineteenth century and has been shown to be less hospitable to Viking ghosts, who prefer ship styles that are closer to the longship (Pegleg, 1987). **(A conclusion sentence shows that the argument has come to a close)** Thus the use of unicorn hair fell out of use by the end of the eighteenth century (Davey-Jones, 2007).

If you know what each paragraph is doing in your essay, you can think about what the reader needs to know, and the most logical order to present this information. We usually don't mind too much if we get the explanation then the evidence, or the other way around, as long as the logical progression is clear.

WORKSHEET 4 // PRACTISE SIGNPOSTING PARAGRAPH MOVES

Now it's time to practise these moves. You can use the question prompts
in this worksheet to help plan out the next essay you are going to write.

What are your ideas for the topic sentence? What's the point of this paragraph?

_____

_____

What step in the argument are you making? In your own words:

_____

_____

What evidence do you have? How will you show your point isn't just your opinion?

_____

_____

_____

_____

How will you use or explain this evidence?

_____

_____

_____

_____

What is coming next?

_____

_____

_____

_____

3.3 FINISHING WELL: THE STRONG CONCLUSION

A conclusion returns to the questions and problems outlined in the first paragraph, the introduction. The purpose of the conclusion is to show you have a strong and convincing argument that answers the questions and problems you decided to tackle.

For a basic conclusion, you could restate the problem, your argument and your solution from the introduction, and just move it into the past tense – 'This essay has argued …' – but to level up your conclusion, you should do more.

The conclusion should revisit the 'moves' you made in the essay and restate your final position. This isn't just repetition. It helps to:

- remind the reader what has happened in a summary, especially if the essay was long or they got interrupted reading it
- enable the reader to check back that you did do what you said you were going to.

But a conclusion has two extra 'moves' that we would expect to see.

1 **Highlight any important limitations to your analysis**. This is especially important in the sciences.
2 **Broaden out to connect your answers to the bigger picture**. This might mean outlining potential for future research, showing how your answer could be implemented in the 'real world', or linking this essay to the previous assessment. These final remarks should be as specific as possible and based on the gaps in the research you have identified.

It is not at all uncommon to write a killer conclusion, then realise that you have included material that belongs in the body of the essay, or that you have set out your argument much more effectively than you did in the introduction. If that happens, don't hide this great writing in the conclusion – use it to rewrite your introduction and then have another go at writing a conclusion. The rule of thumb is: do not introduce any new evidence or ideas in the conclusion.

So, the moves the marker needs to see you make in the conclusion are:

1 Summarise the argument you made.
2 Connect your argument to the 'why' of the essay.
3 Note any limitations in your research or scope.
4 State your final position.

Plus an optional final step you will often see in academic texts:
5 Offer future directions or recommendations.

Getting all these moves squeezed into a paragraph is tricky and takes some practice. A good way to start is to write a sentence or two for each 'move'.

Here's a basic conclusion to our imaginary essay topic:

How should the trade of unicorn hair remedies for plantar fasciitis be regulated so we better preserve this resource for future generations?

(Summarise) In this essay I have shown how the discovery of the use of unicorn hair for treating plantar fasciitis has led to accelerating, worldwide demand for unicorn hair, putting the future of this species at risk. Consumer demand for unicorn hair creates significant problems for regulators tasked

WORKSHEET 5 // PRACTISE CONCLUSION MOVES

Use this space to rough out your conclusion 'moves' using a few prompt questions:

Summarise the argument you made.

_____

_____

_____

Connect your argument to the 'why' of the essay.

_____

_____

_____

Mention any limitations.

_____

_____

_____

State your final position.

_____

_____

_____

Optional: offer future directions or recommendations (but be specific).

_____

_____

_____

WORKSHEET 6 // REVIEW YOUR ENTIRE ESSAY

Once you have written an essay, you might find that you can't see the argument, or that you changed direction. If that's the case, it's not too late. Here are some questions to help you get back on track, or to see the whole essay.

What was the main argument of your essay? Can you capture it in a sentence? Try starting with 'In this essay I argued that ... '

_____

_____

What are the main points of each of your body paragraphs? Can you put them into a single sentence as a list? Try starting with 'In this essay I discussed ... '

_____

_____

_____

_____

How does each of the main points listed above answer the main essay question?

_____

_____

_____

Are there any limitations in the evidence and arguments you have put forward? Any situations or circumstances to which it does not apply?

_____

_____

_____

_____

with maintaining unicorn populations, and farming solutions to produce more to meet demand have so far failed. **(Connect)** There is a clear need for regulators to establish international standards on trade volumes and quality indicators, but the most effective starting point is the establishment of hunter collectives. Hunters' collectives could use local data to agree on appropriate quotas. A global representative body for these collectives could control the amount of unicorn hair traded, region by region. **(Limitation)** This analysis does not take into account the difficulty of getting individual countries to agree to the regulation process or how such a process might be policed. **(Specific future directions)** More research into appropriate regulatory frameworks for structures of hunters' collectives is needed to help save these significant creatures from extinction.

3.4 WRITING LONGER AND LONGER ESSAYS

If you talk to students in later years of their degrees, you might have noticed something alarming. Lecturers begin to ask for longer and longer essays. Just as you are coming to grips with writing a 2000-word essay, you are asked for a 2500-word one. And then a little later they become 3000 words, and it's not unusual at all to need to write at least one 5000-word piece by the end of your degree.

Essays have built-in modules. A longer essay isn't a completely different thing from a short essay – it's just made of more blocks. Each block is a self-sufficient little segment. Each of these modules has a purpose. And you already know how to create these blocks from the section on body paragraphs above (Section 3.2). Here are some tips.

Don't be anxious about writing a longer essay. A longer essay is not necessarily more difficult than a short one. As an advisor of Shaun's once put it, 'The only difference between a 2000-word essay and a 5000-word one is that the latter has more bits in the middle.'

1 Your first module is the introduction

The job of an introduction in a longer essay doesn't change from a shorter piece (see Section 3.1). An introduction should be 10–15 per cent of your essay – possibly more if it includes a context paragraph – so you don't necessarily need a much longer introduction for a longer essay. The only real change you might have to make is in the overview, the section where you say what will be covered in the rest of the essay: perhaps this needs to be a sentence or two longer. But the rest can remain unchanged.

2 Most of the modules in your essay will consist of one or more body paragraphs

Modules are self-contained components of your argument. Earlier in the chapter (Section 3.2), we talked about how body paragraphs contain reasons or premises that support your argument, as a 'chunk of thinking'. Each module paragraph contains the evidence to support one reason. A longer essay just needs more reasons than a shorter one. Alternatively, your reasons can get more nuanced and you can dig a little bit deeper into the reasons. So, while a 2000-word essay might only have space for you to provide three reasons for believing your argument, a 3000-word one might give you space to have five or six.

WORKSHEET 7 // PLAN YOUR ARGUMENT USING PARAGRAPHS

It can be helpful to 'map out' your essay using your argument. Begin with your contention – your hypothesis or claim – then make sure that each paragraph is a step in your argument. You should also keep in mind your word limits, and make sure you have enough room for your evidence and argument.

Use the diagram below to help you practise mapping an argument into an essay plan. For longer essays, or essays with specific instructions, you may have to add more sections.

Each step of the argument has a suggested percentage of the word count. These numbers are a general guide to help you make a judgment about how much information you can plan to include.

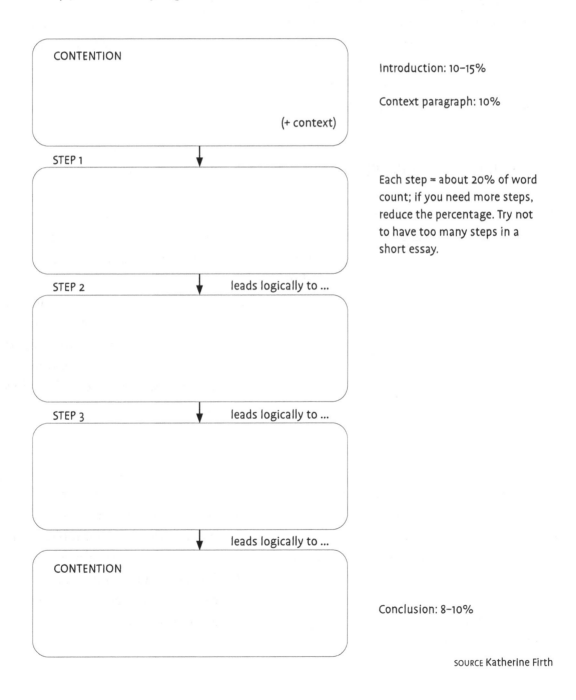

CONTENTION

(+ context)

Introduction: 10–15%

Context paragraph: 10%

STEP 1

Each step = about 20% of word count; if you need more steps, reduce the percentage. Try not to have too many steps in a short essay.

STEP 2   leads logically to ...

STEP 3   leads logically to ...

leads logically to ...

CONTENTION

Conclusion: 8–10%

SOURCE Katherine Firth

Keep this modular format in mind as you do research for your essay. Look at the word length, and work out how many paragraphs/ reasons you can fit in. Then read until you have sufficient information for the number of modules you need.

3 *Conclusions, like introductions, are a single module in your essay*

Conclusions have the same purpose whether they are for a short essay or a long one (see Section 3.3). Like introductions, the only part of the conclusion that needs to be longer is the summary of the body – if you covered more material in the body of the essay, you'll need another sentence or so in the conclusion as well.

3.5 YOUR LEVEL-UP CHECKLIST

We hope you have stopped thinking 'I need to impress with my language' or 'I need to make sure I provide *all* the facts'. The right attitude to a university essay is: 'I need to have a clear and persuasive argument.'

Do:

✓ Clearly explain what your essay is going to cover in the first sentence.
✓ Put a clear statement of your argument in the introduction. Something like 'This essay will argue that ...'
✓ Make sure that your whole essay is focused on moving this argument forward.
✓ Put an outline of what your essay will cover in your introduction, and then order the sections of your essay in the same order.
✓ Use multiple academic sources to support your argument.

✓ Carefully evaluate and explain any evidence that is not from academic sources (see Section 8.1).
✓ Evaluate what your sources have to say.
✓ Synthesise the sources. This means working with partial pieces of evidence and putting enough of these together to make a convincing argument.
✓ Use as many paragraphs as you need within your word limit. There is no standard number of body paragraphs in a university-level essay.
✓ Use your conclusion to offer a summary of your essay and argument to help your reader remember what they have read.

Don't:

✗ Have a descriptive topic sentence as an argument statement. Instead, tell your marker what the essay is about, and also what the essay argues.
✗ Wait until the conclusion to tell the reader what your argument was. Put it in the introduction.
✗ Try to impress with clever language. Keep things simple, and focus on your argument.
✗ Let your sentences get too long. As a general rule, keep to a maximum of 2.5 lines per sentence, or 25–35 words. Remember, if it's more than 40 words long, consider breaking the sentence into two.
✗ Import lots of long quotes into your writing. Instead, paraphrase and explain the idea in your own words.
✗ Rely heavily on a single source and its point of view on your topic. Try to bring together the views of many sources.
✗ Forget to put your own point of view, carefully considered and backed up by all your research.

IN SUMMARY ...

* Every essay should have a beginning, a middle and an end, which all show how your answer to the problem is logical and based on evidence.

* Learn the 'moves' that are expected from each different kind of paragraph or section, and be sure to include them.

* Know why every paragraph is included in your essay, and tell the reader about it in a sentence or two.

4

HOW TO WRITE A CONVINCING ARGUMENT

Argument is what makes a piece of writing an essay rather than a report, a newspaper article, an opinion piece or any other kind of writing.

In Chapter 3 we showed you how to write the three basic sections of an essay: introduction, body and conclusion. This chapter shows you how to put them all together in a way that is logical and coherent. When you achieve this aim, your marker will experience writing that 'flows'.

> Having a single, rigorous, well-presented argument is the most important thing for getting a better grade. When we surveyed rubrics and marking criteria for subjects across disciplines and across universities, it was clear that a strong argument was the most important aspect of moving from a Credit to a Distinction grade. Focusing the argument even more was the best way to move up to a High Distinction.

4.1 WHAT ARGUMENTS LOOK LIKE (AND WHAT THEY DON'T)

As we said in Chapter 2, an academic argument is not a fight! It doesn't involve shouting, violence or crying. An argument in an essay should rely on the weight of the evidence being presented, not the strength of feeling on both sides.

> An *academic argument* is a connected set of reasons offered to support an idea, action or theory.

Academic arguments are rooted in classic logic, where you state 'premises' that lead to one or more 'conclusions':

Premise 1:   When the pipes leak, the water pressure falls.

Premise 2:   The pipes are leaking.

Conclusion: The water pressure has fallen.

When we say 'your own position' or 'your point of view', what we really mean is 'your logical conclusion that you drew from the evidence, shown in the premises'. So, a good argument:

1   offers a point of view, then
2   provides reasons for that point of view.

Your reasons must be properly supported by scholarly evidence. The reasons must be based in research, and in the points of view of other scholars in your field. The reasons should *not* be based on your opinion or how you feel about the topic.

In an academic argument, you state your point of view – your 'conclusion' – *before* your reasons! Once your reader knows you think the water pressure has fallen, they will listen out for your reasons and evidence, and see if they think these are convincing enough. Don't forget that essays rarely have a right or wrong answer – just stronger and weaker arguments.

Why you have to take a side

When you learned essay writing at high school or elsewhere, you might not have been taught to take a position and argue for it. High school teachers often expect essays that have a balanced conclusion – where you say something like 'both sides have merit'. One of the big challenges for high school teachers is to help students to think through complex ideas with multiple sides. Rather than encouraging you to jump to a conclusion, your teachers may have taught you to stop and look at both sides first. The advantage of this training is that it enables you to identify different arguments.

For a university essay, you still need to weigh up the different sides, but you do that *before* you start writing. By the time you write your introduction, you should be ready to state your position. We want to know what side won you over, and why.

In order to have a 'strong' argument, you need to make the case for your position. If you don't have a position, you can't make a case for it! If your argument is divided between two equal positions ('on the one hand … on the other'), you have effectively split your argument in half – making two weak arguments, not one strong one.

Deciding which side to take

In your research, while listening to lectures and when taking part in tutorial conversations, you should be looking out for the different positions people hold. They might disagree radically, or they might just hold slightly different opinions.

Once you have identified different positions, you should then group them. You could make a list, or maybe get out the books and articles and stack them into piles of people who agree with each other.

Now you need to take it deeper.

Why do you think these people agree/ disagree with each other?
- Do they share a theoretical or philosophical position?
- Did the scholarly consensus change over time? What new approach or evidence caused that change?
- What is the purpose of their research? Do theoretical research and applied research have different approaches?
- Are there other reasons?

Once you know what other people think, and you have a good idea why they think it, it's time to take a position. *What do you think?*

You have access to lots of information. You have data, you have primary sources, you have the advice of experts (lecturers, the authors of the articles you are reading). You can use this information to help you take a position.

Many questions have been settled by lots of researchers doing lots of research over a long period of time. This process is called reaching a 'scholarly consensus'. Usually, an undergraduate will not have access to enough information to credibly contest consensus. For example, if 97 per cent of actively publishing climate scientists agree that climate change is real and impacted by human activities, then it's clear that you should agree with them! Likewise, just go with Shakespeare not being the Earl of Oxford and the world not being flat. Taking a contrarian view is very risky; only do it if you see an emerging group of expert scholars with new and *credible* ideas. (Hint: One geologist saying climate change is not real is not as credible as 1000 climatologists saying it is real.)

In some other cases, however, you will have read and heard multiple interpretations that all seem valid, to a greater or lesser degree. This is the moment to use your critical judgment. Which interpretation seems to you to have the strongest evidence? Which position enables you to dive deepest into the question? Is there a way of bringing two interpretations together to make a more nuanced, blended account?

It's likely you will find one side of an argument more persuasive than another. You will express yourself more clearly and find the essay easier to write if you know *why* you find that side of the argument more attractive. Perhaps your reasons are pragmatic, perhaps ethical, perhaps aesthetic. Lean into it!

It can help to ask yourself some questions:

- Will focusing on this dimension give you skills in a job you would like to do later?
- Does this subject align with your values?
- Or are you passionate about the content for other reasons?

Which of the potential positions is most useful to you as an emerging economist, or a budding poet, or a developing social worker? Linking your essays to your goals is motivating and tends to lead to better grades.

4.2   USING TRUTH CLAIMS

If your lecturer wanted to test you on the facts, they would set a different kind of assignment, like a series of multiple-choice questions or a short-answer test. Essays are for situations where you need to move beyond statements of fact to evaluate the evidence. Your evaluation is expressed as a series of 'truth claims'.

What is a truth claim?

> A truth claim is simply a statement of what you think is true about a situation, circumstance or object. A truth claim in an academic essay should always be backed up by reasons and evidence.

Here's a totally made-up example showing the difference between a statement of fact and a truth claim:

Statement of fact: People in Australia farm unicorns for their magical hair.

Truth claim: Unicorns are critical to the economic prosperity of Australia.

A person only needs to see a field full of unicorns to accept the statement of fact above as true. If a person is to accept the truth claim about the role of unicorns in economic prosperity, they need reasons and evidence.

You only need one truth claim to build an essay, but you can make multiple truth claims if you like. Ideally, truth claims build on, or complement, each other in successive body paragraphs. In fact, a good way to map out an essay is to write a list of related truth claims you think you can support with reasons and evidence, like so:

- Farmers want to have more unicorns than sheep on their farms.

- Unicorns produce longer horns when fed magical fodder.

- Elves and dwarves should be paid for their role in blessing unicorn fodder.

But remember, the more truth claims you have, the more complex your argument will be. You might not have enough room in a short essay to give enough supportive evidence. If in doubt, stick to one meaty truth claim!

Someone else writing on the same essay topic as you can make different truth claims. They might even take the opposite position. From the marker's point of view, as long as the arguments you use to support your truth claim(s) are defensible, you can both still get a good mark.

Turn a truth claim into a question

Some lecturers like you to write your own essay questions. A well-written essay question helps you to think about what you are supposed to be

Table 1: Generating an essay question

Strategy	Example essay question	Example position you can take in this essay
Add a question word like 'how', 'why' or 'to what extent'	To what extent were unicorns critical to the economic prosperity of the state of New South Wales in the 1880s?	Unicorns were less critical to the economic prosperity of New South Wales than pixies.
Find a scholar who makes a truth claim, quote their point of view and add a discussion prompt.	'Unicorns were critical to the economic prosperity of the state of New South Wales in the 1880s' (Yksisarvinen, 2002). Discuss.	Yksisarvinen has argued that 'unicorns were critical to the economic prosperity of the state of New South Wales in the 1880s' (2002), but Aon-Adharcach (2018) has argued that pixies were even more significant.
Set up a problem raised by the truth claim.	If unicorns were critical to the economic prosperity of the state of New South Wales in the 1880s, why were there so few unicorn farms?	There were few unicorn farms because unicorns made only a small contribution to the New South Wales economy in the 1880s. There were many pixie farms because pixies were more critical.
Notice where the limits of the truth claim sit and ask a question beyond it.	Unicorns were critical to the economic prosperity of the state of New South Wales in the 1880s. Why did this change in the 1890s?	By 1889, farmers and politicians had realised that the economic value of unicorn hair had been overestimated. From 1890, a change in rhetoric mirrored this new understanding.
Put the truth claim together with a theory.	Critically evaluate the Vienradzis theory of why unicorns were critical to the economic prosperity of the state of New South Wales in the 1880s.	Vienradzis (1965) argues that economic value is measured more by prestige than by financial contribution. While her theory explains the position taken by Yksisarvinen (2002), it does not account for the criticisms levelled by Aon-Adharcach (2018).

WORKSHEET 8 // PRACTISE TRUTH CLAIMS

Now practise turning statements of fact into truth claims. Here are a few
sentence skeletons to help get you started drafting some questions of your own.

Critically evaluate [a situation, event or proposal] using theories or evidence from [a place, time, organisation or person].

Discuss the difference between [situation 1] and [situation 2] in terms of [analytical approach].

Examine whether [proposal] is important/valuable/relevant in light of [existing situation].

Compare and contrast the relative strengths of [example 1] and [example 2] in [situation].

Did [event] impact the transition of [entity] after [time period] to [new situation]?

To what degree did [person] contribute to the development of [situation]?

Strategy	Example essay question	Example position you can take in this essay
Add a question word like 'how', 'why' or 'to what extent'.		
Find a scholar who makes a truth claim, quote their point of view and add a discussion prompt.		
Set up a problem raised by the truth claim.		
Notice where the limits of the truth claim sit and ask a question beyond it.		
Put the truth claim together with a theory.		

learning by including lots of clues about what to research, how to research it and why you are researching it.

You can turn truth claims into an essay question quite easily. For example:

> *Truth claim:* Unicorns were critical to the economic prosperity of the state of New South Wales in the 1880s.

Already, we have a number of embedded premises, theories, topics and methods in the statement. We are looking at the:

- **topic** of unicorns
- **region** of New South Wales (a state in Australia)
- **period** of the 1880s
- **theories** of how financial value is created
- **methods** of historical and economic research
- **techniques** like document analysis and economic modelling.

There's a handy table format on page 41 to help you generate a range of questions from a basic truth claim like the one above.

4.3 FIND YOUR ESSAY STRUCTURE WITHIN THE QUESTION

You can 'discover the structure' of your essay by closely examining the verbs in the questions. Here are some common verbs and ideas for forms.

1 *'Compare and contrast' questions*

Questions that ask you to *compare and contrast* are quite common. They involve picking at least two things: for example, unicorns and pixies; building freight boats or fishing boats; the ideas of Yksisarvinen (2002) and Aon-Adharcach (2018).

You are expected to look at how they are similar ('compare') and how they are different ('contrast'). You should definitely present more than one position in these essays but remember that you need to have a critical position: one side should be more compelling than the other.

There are three main ways of handling a compare-and-contrast question.

- Split the essay into two not-quite-even halves. Pick one side/thing/example, explain it. Then, pick the other side/thing/example, show how it is similar and different to the first. Usually, you pick the stronger example to go second.
- Start with talking about how things are similar ('compare'); then spend the second half of the essay talking about how they are different ('contrast').
- Identify the most important points that are common across both examples. Tackle each sub-topic in turn, comparing and contrasting both examples. The conclusion then summarises the reasons why one is better than another.

Whichever strategy you take, you can see how the sections of the essay would progress logically in order.

2 *Yes/No questions*

Yes/No questions ask you to decide whether or not something is correct. Don't be tempted to avoid coming to a conclusion. For example, if the question is:

> Did World War II adversely impact Australia's trade relationships in the Pacific after 1945?

The answer can't be 'Maybe?' or 'Who knows?'.

Offer a clear argument statement that shows the answer you will be supporting. From there, the paragraphs or sections of your essay should each handle one specific aspect, or one piece of evidence you have for taking that point of view.

3 'To what degree' questions

'To what degree' questions are an extension of the yes/no format. Here, in addition to needing to argue whether something is, or is not, the case, you must also put forward a sub-argument about how strongly this seems to be so, and why.

For example, consider this question:

To what degree should non-steroidal anti-inflammatory drugs be a first choice for treating dental pain?

Here, you would first need to argue whether these drugs are a first choice or not. You would then need to push the argument further by making a case for them being a clear preference, or just one among many.

4 'Discuss' questions

'Discuss' questions are often a favourite with students because they seem softer than more direct argumentation questions, but this is an illusion! These types of questions still require you to take a point of view on the topic of discussion, and in fact can be trickier to structure and argue.

'Discuss' questions sometimes use verbs like 'examine', 'analyse' or even 'describe'. Confusingly, no matter which verb is used, you should *not* present two equal sides or write down a description of the situation.

There are two basic strategies:

1   You could just decide to treat it like a 'compare and contrast', a 'yes/no' or a 'to what degree' question.
2   Alternatively, you might decide that you are being asked to come to a conclusion about what is and isn't known about your topic. Your argument is then about the state of knowledge in the area. In science subjects, an essay called 'review and synthesis' is often requesting this approach.

For example:

Discuss the slowing of birth rates in developing countries.

If you decided to use a 'to what degree' strategy, your argument could be something like:

This essay will argue that while there is a general trend of declining birth rates in developing nations, there are some notable exceptions to this pattern.

Alternatively, you could take the approach of writing an argument about the state of knowledge about birth rates:

Inconsistencies in data collection across developing countries mean that it is difficult to make accurate comparisons between countries, particularly where there are limited official health systems in remote or rural areas.

'Discuss' questions give you the flexibility to decide the best question style to address the aspect of the topic that interests you. But whatever you do, you must pick a question and then organise your information logically.

4.4 ORGANISE YOUR INFORMATION WITH LATCH

Sometimes it can be tricky to decide how to structure your essay in a logical way. One way to approach your essay structure is to use the 'LATCH' theory of information by Richard Saul Wurman, from the book *Information Anxiety 2*. You can use LATCH to organise your research notes or literature, and then to organise your essay structure.

LATCH stands for:
- **Location**: could be geographical, spatial or cultural
- **Alphabetical**: just what it sounds like
- **Time**: as a sequence, usually forward or backward
- **Category**: sorted by type (styles, colour, political party)
- **Hierarchy**: sorted by value (best to worst, biggest to smallest, most important to least important).

If you use **Location,** arrange all the information you collect by the region, country, place, situation or location it relates to. Discuss one location, then discuss another.

You are unlikely to use **Alphabetical** information inside your essay, except to structure the reference list, which will be ordered by the first letter in the family name of the author. You might also use alphabetical order to arrange information within tables or figures.

Time is particularly useful as a way to organise an essay. Many arts and humanities subjects divide up their degree by periods, so time is a natural way to structure your essay. But there are plenty of other reasons to use

time as an ordering device. Once you have sequenced your information appropriately you can start writing: 'first this happened, then that happened'. Sometimes you can use time not just to describe what order things happened in, but to suggest causation: 'this happened, therefore that happened next'.

Category is one of the most flexible structures; think about category as a theme or group where things contain similar features. While putting things into categories is helpful to create clarity, it can be difficult to use it to structure an argument. Be careful about relying on Category too much as it tends to make all the data in a group look the same. It also encourages you to put things in separate compartments, so they don't obviously connect. If you use categories, also make sure to clearly show the relationships between them that can help you explain what it all can mean. (You might do this by also using Hierarchy.)

The H stands for **Hierarchy**: organising information from best to worse, most to least, highest to lowest, most important to least important, biggest to smallest and so on. Arranging information by hierarchy can help you make an argument more easily because it helps you make value judgments. Hierarchy is embedded in many questions, such as 'to what degree' and 'what were the most important aspects of' kinds of questions.

4.5 STRUCTURE YOUR WRITING WITH DIAGRAMS

Diagrams can help you capture your ideas and move them around before you have to commit them to long-form text. In a diagram you can view your ideas from a great height so that you can see the relationships and connections, rather than all the detail that can obscure your argument. These two aspects make diagrams

WORKSHEET 9 // USE LATCH TO ORGANISE IDEAS

These diagrams will help you use LATCH to organise your ideas.
You can print or photocopy them as templates, populate them with information
from your research for the essay and then turn them into a visual plan for your writing.

L is for Location

T is for Time

Each box or circle represents a date on the timeline, with space to add text for each one.

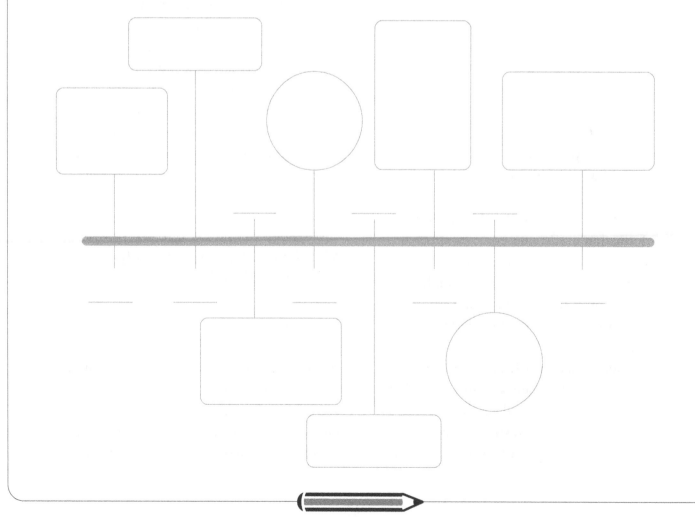

WORKSHEET 9 // USE LATCH TO ORGANISE IDEAS

C is for Category

This diagram helps you lay out all your reasons and associated evidence in a tree format so you can see them all on the same page. This can be used as a writing aid to figure out everything that needs to be in your essay.

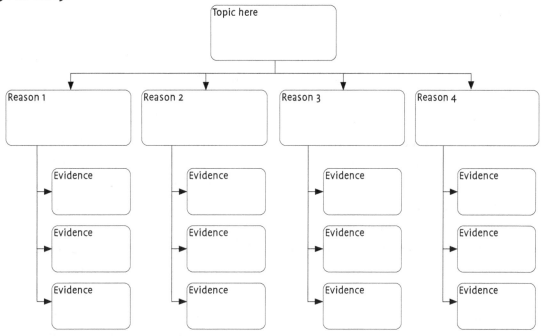

H is for Hierarchy

This diagram is similar to the category diagram above, but encourages you to 'stack' the reasons in order of importance. This can be used as a writing aid to sequence the reasons you present to support your argument in your essay. You can write from left to right, or right to left.

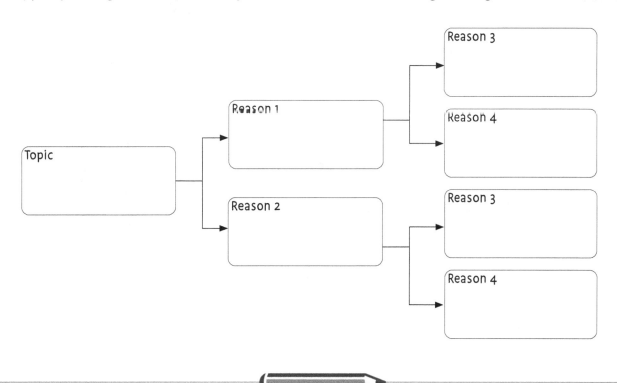

a great way to plan out the structure of your essay, to map out what an essay question is telling you to do, or to work out where you lost your way in the research and writing stages.

This section introduces you to a couple of different diagram types, with a suggested sequence for using them.

The best way to map out your writing with a diagram is on a whiteboard – it is very easy to rub out and change diagrams on a whiteboard and you can use a phone camera to capture the ideas and keep them with you while you write. Often you can use a whiteboard in a study room or classroom on campus if you don't have one at home. We have also given you some space on the following pages to draw your own versions, or you can use mind-mapping software: a simple online search will show you a lot of free programs you can use.

Feather diagram

The feather diagram is a good structured brainstorming technique to use at the beginning of your essay-writing process.

It's good for capturing many ideas and starting to organise them. This diagram will help you generate lots of ideas – more than you can deal with in a short piece of writing.

If you aren't sure about the best way to approach an essay question, a feather diagram is a good way to try out a couple of different essay plans quickly, and then compare them to decide which is the best. You could even take your feather diagrams along to your lecturer in their office hours and get advice on which approach they think will be most effective.

Note: If you already know how you plan to approach an essay, you are better off using a fishbone diagram (see next section, page 50).

To make a feather diagram:

1 Draw a circle and write a sentence capturing the area you want to explore.
2 Draw out a spine that represents a category that relates to the topic area.
3 On each spine, draw out a number of smaller lines that represent further areas of exploration related to the topic.

Figure 1: Feather diagram

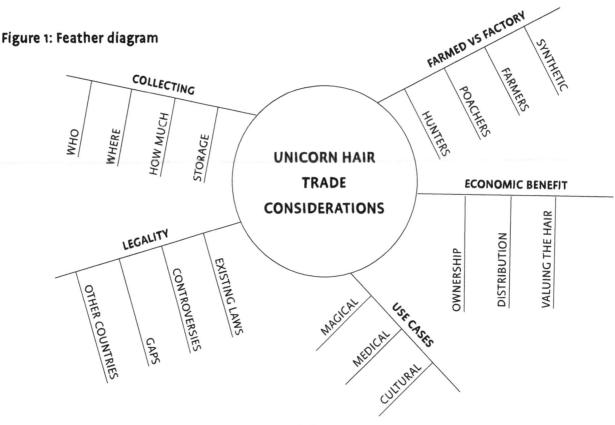

This is a space for you to try out your own feather diagram.

Fishbone diagram

The Ishikawa cause-and-effect diagram, often called a fishbone diagram, is best used when you already know the question or problem but you need to work out what contributed to causing the problem, and how you might solve it. The diagram was developed by Japanese business innovator Kaoru Ishikawa (1972), a pioneer of quality-control processes. A fishbone diagram is a good way to arrange information for 'state of knowledge' essay structures where you have to analyse cause and effect, as in our example below:

To make a fishbone diagram:

1 Draw the fish 'head' on the right hand side of your page and write the situation you want to explore inside it.
2 Then draw a 'backbone' or spine, connected to the head with an arrow.
3 Identify between three and five causes that could be leading to the problem and draw these as fishbones connected to the spine.
4 Label each of the causes at the end of each fishbone.
5 Brainstorm around each cause for any explanations you can think of, and add them to smaller bones. Try to come up with as many of these smaller bones as you can.

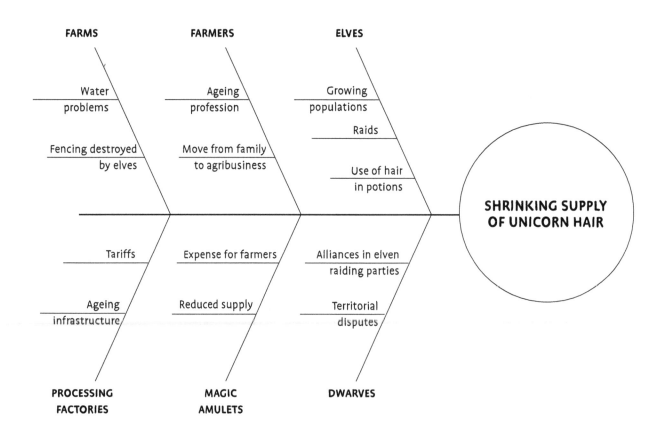

Figure 2: Fishbone diagram

This is a space for you to try out your own fishbone diagram.

Spider diagram

Spider diagrams help you to plan your essay visually. You will decide on the hierarchy, and then fill in the details. A spider diagram helps you to see the relationships between the different paragraphs too.

To make a spider diagram:

1   Start with your essay question in the centre bubble.
2   Draw between three and five 'legs' coming out from your centre bubble. Write the most important themes or causes in these circles – each of these bubbles represents a potential paragraph of your essay.
3   Draw more legs out from these bubbles to start filling in more details – this can be other research articles or reports you want to cite, facts, statistics and ideas that will go in each paragraph.

You can take a photo of your finished spider diagram and put it at the top of your essay document to remind you of what you want to write as you go.

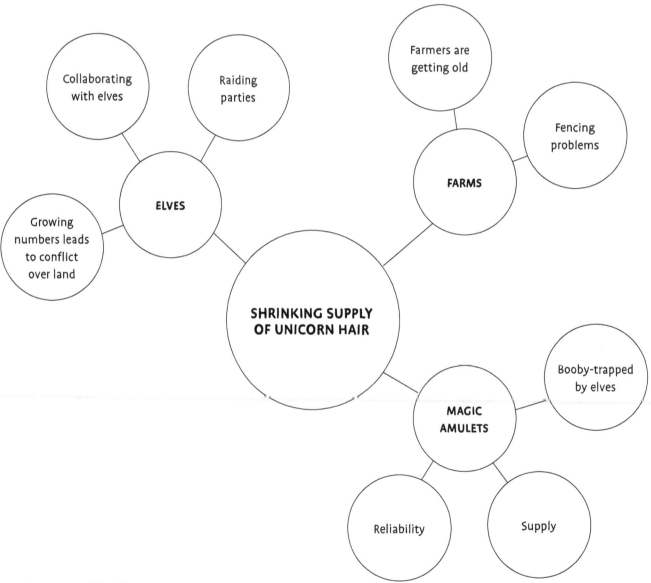

Figure 3: Spider diagram

WORKSHEET 12 // SPIDER DIAGRAM

This is a space for you to try out your own spider diagram.

Quadrant diagram

Quadrant diagrams are another way to map out your argument, for people who like neat squares rather than free bubbles.

To make a quadrant diagram:

1 On a large piece of paper or a whiteboard, draw a square with the essay question in it, then surround it with four equally sized squares.
2 Take the best three reasons that support your argument and write them in three of the quadrants – these are your premises for the topic.
3 Use the rest of the space in each quadrant to record all the authors and bits of evidence you have collected in note form.
4 In the fourth quadrant, put the key counter-arguments that people could use to dispute your positions.
5 Keep the diagram close as you write the essay, working on each premise in turn. This is very useful in subjects where you need to write defensively, like law. Remember to address both the strengths of your own argument but also refute any potential counter-arguments.

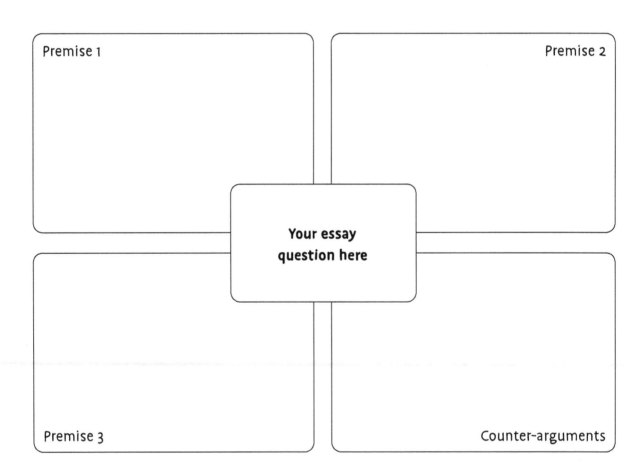

Figure 4: Quadrant diagram

SOURCE Credit to Alexandra Horden, who shared this method with Inger and swears it got her a Distinction or higher in every essay she wrote in law school

WORKSHEET 13 // QUADRANT DIAGRAM

This is a space for you to try out your own quandrant diagram.

4.6 USE SENTENCE SKELETONS TO STATE YOUR ARGUMENTS

Just as there are specific structures for the typical research essay question styles, so there are typical ways to frame your answers in language. You can think about this like an accent in spoken language. Knowing what these language structures are and how to use them will help you to write out your arguments in ways that sound 'academic', because they follow academic language patterns.

One of our favourite techniques is Swales and Feak's (1994) 'sentence skeletons'. These are 'fill-in-the-blanks' sentences that shape your writing into an academic style. The tactic is surprisingly simple: if you like how the piece of writing works, strip the paragraph of the content and reuse the structure.

Consider the following body paragraph from a totally made-up essay on unicorn hair:

> Unicorn hair was widely used in the eighteenth century for dealing with ghosts, as Louise Pegleg has argued in her foundational anthropological monograph, *Unicorns and Ghosts* (1987). One of the most common uses was to deal with Viking ghosts (Egyszarvú, 2012; Njëbrirësh, 1991), and one of the rarest uses was to encourage cleanliness in village wells (Topsail, 1995, p. 129; see further Topsail, 1998). This essay will compare two published diaries by magic practitioners based near Portsmouth between 1700 and 1800: Sara Dubloon (1720–30) and Duncan Polly (1785–90).

Stripped of content, it looks like this:

> _____ was widely used for dealing with _____, as [author] has argued in [insert publication here]. One of the most common uses was _____, and one of the rarest uses was _____. This essay will compare [two ideas, publications or sources].

Now we can adapt this sentence skeleton for an entirely new (also made-up) topic. The technique works best when you freely write over the structure and discard any parts that don't work for the new topic. Think about it as 'riffing' on the original, rather than remaking it exactly as it was before, like this (the original text is shown in bold):

> Minotaur hoof extract **was widely used for dealing with** a range of skin conditions in children, as shown in the scientific study by Sorkat and Picioare (2009). **One of the most common uses was** to deal with warts, **and one of the rarest reasons was** bunions. **This essay will compare** the merits of Minotaur hooves over modern artificial compounds.

The advantage of this technique is that it defeats the blank page and helps you start formulating an academic voice without working entirely from scratch. As you read, copy any really good 'skeletons' you see to use later. Or you can use a book like Luiz Otávio Barros's *The Only Academic Phrasebook You'll Ever Need*, which has many examples.

You might be a bit worried about making and using sentence skeletons because of the risk of plagiarism: however, phrases like 'this essay will compare', or 'as [author] has argued' are too common to 'belong' to another author. If you are borrowing skeletons from many different sources, then remixing them and adapting them to your own sentences, then they will start to become your sentences.

We said in the introduction that academic writing at university is often plain.

These sentences help you to write the clear, straightforward, technical kinds of sentences that get good marks.

4.7 HOW TO 'USE THEORY'

Many assignments will expect you to 'use theory' in your research essays. A theory is a rigorous approach to thinking, or a framework for explaining observations. Such a theory obviously gives you another technique to build a 'logical' structure for your essay.

A theory might be something used so often you don't even notice it – the 'scientific method' is a theory that provides a framework for making hypotheses, testing them through experimentation and drawing conclusions. This is why a science or psychology report uses a structure of 'Introduction, Methods, Results, Discussion', which is different from the 'Introduction, Body, Conclusion' essay structure we talked about in Chapter 3.

A theory may be associated with a 'theorist', like Sigmund Freud, Judith Butler or Albert Einstein. In Sutton and Staw's article 'What theory is not' (1995), they point out that including lots of references to theoreticians, or even including a long description of their theories in your essay, is not the same as 'using theory'.

Instead, theories predict why certain things will happen the way they do. For example, a *scientific theory* about gravity predicts what will happen if you drop a ball on Earth versus what will happen if you drop it on the Moon. A sociological *narrative theory* attempts to provide explanations of why people behave the way they do. For example, game theory suggests people are locked in a competitive struggle against each other; the job of the researcher is to work out what power moves and counter-moves people make to win, and to describe them.

Other theories are more earth shaking: they try to change what kind of question you can ask, what kinds of evidence you can use, how you can interpret the results or even how something becomes real. For example, Indigenous knowledge theories use non-Western forms of logic, evidence and hierarchies (see Paul DiMaggio, 'Comments on "What theory is not"', 1995).

If you are a first-year undergraduate, you are not expected to go out and find your own theory. You will usually be taught about the theories in class, so just make sure you 'use' the theories – don't just describe or reference them. Once you have named the theory and briefly explained how it works, you should then apply it to your data. Depending on the theory, you should use it to explain why a problem or situation exists, predict outcomes, propose solutions or raise new questions. Follow the logical steps, assumptions and limitations of your theory in setting out your argument and deciding what to focus on. Don't forget to restate your theoretical argument in the introduction and conclusion!

IN SUMMARY ...

* Use your argument, the essay question, and your information organisation as structuring devices for your essay.

* An argument has evidence to back up a truth claim, not just feelings or opinions.

* Use recognised words, sentence structures and theories to write essay questions and essay answers.

* Use these argument-planning techniques in ways that work for you. Some people think visually; others like to work in the linear world of the text. Be prepared to try different ways of working to see what might help you.

PART 2

COMMON PROBLEMS AND
HOW TO FIX THEM

You don't need to read Part 2 straightaway, or not all of it. We suggest you dip in and out of the different kinds of advice we give here, as and when you need it. If you are struggling with words and sentences, with writing academic English, with editing, with research and note taking, or with time management and planning ... then jump straight to the section you need, get the lowdown and get back to writing.

This section is also really helpful to read after you get feedback on an assignment. If a lecturer tells you that you have issues with the 'passive voice', were 'too colloquial', or write in a 'woolly' way, then we have a bite-sized explainer that helps you crack the code and move on to the next stage.

If you have skipped ahead straight to this Part, we also recommend heading back to the first four chapters, since they focus on the challenges that have the biggest implications for grades. If you don't have an argument in your research essay, you can't get a Distinction, no matter how good your time management or grammar is!

5

FOCUSING ON YOUR WORDS AND SENTENCES

You now understand the purpose of essays and how they get marked. You have an idea how to structure your essay into sections, and how to make a coherent, logical, academic argument. So now it's time to get down to the word-by-word level.

> People tend to think 'good grammar' is the same as 'good writing'. It isn't. We've told you to write in a clear, concise and accurate way, rather than showing off your fancy vocabulary.

Make sure your argument is structured in a clear way and highlighted throughout the essay. Focus more on explaining your ideas and showing you understand complex content. Then do a quick spelling and grammar check at the end.

You might be someone who finds it easy to bash out a first draft, but you find it hard to rewrite your text to make it clear and academic. Or you might find the idea of writing and rewriting so overwhelming that you avoid writing at all – or at least put it off until the very last minute. We have advice in Chapters 5–7 on how to edit, and some advice for planning your time and writing a messy first draft in Chapter 9.

For an essay of up to a few thousand words, it doesn't matter much if you write fast and then revise, or write slowly and revise as you go. You will still need revision tools to make your words better.

Before you get too deeply worried about word choice or grammar issues, focus on the big picture: your structure, content, and expression or style. Because these are bigger picture issues, they generally have a bigger impact on your grade.

There are many 'norms' around how essays should look and feel. Dealing with these conventions can be tricky, because they are mostly unspoken. There is also disagreement between different subjects, or different countries, on what 'good' academic writing looks like.

If you aren't sure about how to put together your essay, ask your lecturer or the writing centre at your university for examples of good essays. Even better, if they have time ask them to explain to you what makes those essays good.

> Have a look at two or more examples of good essays in your subject area. What do they have in common? Try to produce those features in your own writing.

It would take us ten books to tease out all the complexities of language use, so let's just look at some common stumbling blocks.

5.1   SHOULD I USE 'I'?

Many academic styles encourage an impersonal tone. In some styles this means completely avoiding the word 'I'. For example, a scientist writing a methods section would rarely say:

> I extracted the protein from the unicorn hair because I thought it would be a good way of guessing the age of the animal.

Instead, they would show that their method would be valid regardless of the person using it and say:

> The protein was extracted from a sample of unicorn hair to test the validity of using protein markers to assess the age of each animal.

Or they might use the royal 'we' to indicate that a group of people all did something the same way:

> We extracted the protein from a sample of unicorn hair to test the validity of using protein markers to assess the age of each animal.

Other disciplines are much more accepting about the use of the word 'I', but even in disciplines that do occasionally use 'I', it is very limited: for example, only for phrases like 'In this essay I will argue … '. It is very uncommon for you to be able to get away with phrases like 'I think … '.

Sometimes a sentence will get really awkward to write because you are trying so hard to get rid of the 'I'. In those cases, check out the advice later in this chapter about the passive voice – or accept that this is a situation where writing a clear sentence is more important than not using 'I'.

5.2   GET YOUR SENTENCES STRAIGHT

A sentence in English needs to contain only two things: a *subject* and a *verb* – that is, a thing and what it does. The subject always goes before the verb.

> The dog runs.

> Ellis runs.

> I run.

This is different from other languages like German or Latin.

In English, the subject mostly goes at the beginning of the sentence, or at least at the beginning of the main clause. A *clause* is a section of a sentence. Clauses are usually separated by a comma or by a joining word like 'and', 'or', 'but'.

You can also have a much longer sentence. Let's break one down for you– see Table 2 opposite.

Table 2: The grammar of a sentence

In English,	This is a dependent clause. It adds extra detail or information, but you could delete it and still have a useful sentence. There is no subject or verb here.	Notice how the clause is separated from the rest of the sentence by a comma?
the subject mostly goes at the beginning of the sentence	This is the main clause, because it has both the subject and the verb.	Here the subject is literally 'the subject'! The verb is 'goes'.
, or at least at the beginning of the main clause.	This is another dependent clause, again adding extra detail. Again, the subject and verb aren't here.	Again, the comma shows that this is an extra bit of sentence.

So now we have all the tools we need to write sentences that are easy to read. We know we need:

- a subject
- a verb
- for the subject and the verb to be near the beginning of the sentence
- for there to be one main clause
- for there to be extra detail in dependent clauses, but maybe we'll need to delete some.

Here are some typical reasons why sentences are considered difficult to read, and how to fix them so they help the reader understand what you mean!

Too many dependent clauses

When we speak, we often use 'run on' sentences, with lots of clauses. When we write, usually one main clause and one dependent clause is plenty. When you have three or more dependent clauses, it gets very hard to follow the sentence.

The best way to break down the sentence is to reduce the number of clauses. We can delete information if we think it's irrelevant, or we can use it to make new sentences.

For example, this (totally made-up) sentence has **three subjects**, lots of connector words, and *multiple verbs*:

These two diarists *demonstrate* the ways that **unicorn hair** *was* not simply instrumental for the practitioners, but *had* a range of **religious meanings** which *developed* from purity and virginity symbols in the earlier part of the century to sacrificial symbols from 1775.

It would be much simpler to break the sentence down into three shorter sentences.

These two diarists *demonstrate* the ways that unicorn hair was not simply instrumental for the practitioners. **The unicorn hair** *had* a range of religious meanings. **The religious meanings** *developed* from purity and virginity symbols in the earlier part of the century to sacrificial symbols from 1775.

Confusing or unclear subject

These two diarists demonstrate the ways that unicorn hair was not simply instrumental for the practitioners, but had a range of religious meanings which developed after 1775.

In this terrible example sentence, we refer back to something we had mentioned previously using words like 'these' and 'which'. In such a complicated sentence, it can be hard to remember or work out what we were talking about, so the reader might have to go backward and reread the sentence or paragraph.

It's better to repeat the name or thing again. It might be boring, but it's less confusing:

> <u>Dubloon and Polly</u> demonstrate the ways that unicorn hair was not simply instrumental for the practitioners, but had a range of religious meanings. <u>The religious meanings</u> developed …

In university essays, we don't care as much about repetition as we do about accuracy. For ESL students who learned to write for the IELTS test, and anyone who paid attention in high school English, this may come as a surprise. University-level academic writing is more interested in following your ideas than testing a large vocabulary.

Your sentence is too long

You can read a sentence aloud for about 25–35 words – obviously depending on how many syllables there are in each word, and a few other variables. Even when we read silently, many people move their lips and tongue as if they were speaking the words; or sound out the words in their head, unconsciously waiting to breathe at the full stop. If your sentences are too long, you will leave your readers breathless!

This example sentence, used earlier, is 42 words long:

> These two diarists demonstrate the ways that unicorn hair was not simply instrumental for the practitioners, but had a range of religious meanings which developed from purity and virginity symbols in the earlier part of the century to sacrificial symbols from 1775.

The easiest way to split it up is to divide it in half:

> These two diarists demonstrate the ways that unicorn hair was not simply instrumental for the practitioners, but had a range of religious meanings. (23 words)

> The range of meanings developed from purity and virginity symbols in the earlier part of the century to sacrificial symbols from 1775. (22 words).

Or you could decide that you don't need all of the detail in this sentence, as you explain the ideas fully later in the essay. So you could delete some of the less relevant information:

> These two diarists demonstrate the ways that unicorn hair was both instrumental and had a range of religious meanings from purity to sacrificial symbols. (24 words).

Often, just reading your sentence aloud shows you how to fix it, even if you can't remember all the grammar rules.

Recap! A sentence should:
- ideally have fewer than 25–35 words
- Have a main clause, and perhaps a dependent clause
- Have the subject and the verb near the beginning
- Re-use names and nouns to avoid needing to refer back
- Finish with a full stop
- Be written with the reader in mind.

5.3 SIGNPOSTING LANGUAGE

You need to lead your reader through your argument smoothly and in a way that doesn't make reading and marking difficult. Even when you aren't the most naturally gifted writer, there are some simple writing tricks that make your writing clearer.

One of the best tools for helping a reader navigate your essay is 'signposting language'. As the name suggests, the job of a signpost is to point the reader in the direction that you plan to take your essay. Here are the most high-impact signposting tricks to make your work easy to read.

1 Signposting the argument

The single most important piece of signposting in any essay is the signpost that tells the reader what the argument is. There should be a clear statement of your academic point of view. This helps the reader understand the context for the evidence you will be presenting in your essay. You might have been taught that stating your argument so bluntly is 'inelegant', but a university essay is more about clear communication.

For example:

This essay will argue that *Star Wars* was one of the most important mythologies of the twentieth century.

In this essay I will demonstrate that Jones *et al.* (2010) overestimated the impact of the anti-vax movement as a result of a poor reading of the data available to them.

I take the position that despite being rarely implemented in modern phylogenetic studies, parsimony methods have distinct benefits over common implementations of maximum likelihood.

If you find that you haven't worked out your argument or position clearly until the conclusion, make sure you rewrite the introduction and any content paragraphs to include it.

2 Signposting the content of the essay

Making your work easy to read is about managing the mental energy of your reader, so it is also important to lay out what will happen in your essay, and in what order. Just like an in-game map is really helpful to stop you getting lost as you navigate around a new world, so an outline of an essay gives your reader some clues about how to follow your progress through your research. If the reader doesn't know what's going to happen and in what order, they will need to spend their mental energy figuring out the structure of your essay, and they might make wrong turns.

The usual place for telling the reader what is going to happen is just after the argument statement in the introduction. For example:

This essay will argue that, as far as morality is concerned, *Star Wars* was one of the most important mythologies of the twentieth century. **I will first give an overview of** popular mythologies in the twentieth century, **then position** *Star Wars* as one of these mythologies, and **finally demonstrate that** the morality stories of *Star Wars* have penetrated more deeply into the popular consciousness of American and Australian cinema-goers than any other mythology of the twentieth century.

As you can see, we have clearly laid out what will be covered, and the order in which these things will be covered. The example not only explains the kinds of content ('overview', 'position') but also the content of the argument. Don't write:

> **I will first** review the background, **then describe** the case study and **finally demonstrate** my conclusion.

Make sure that the body of your essay then moves through its topics in the order given. Do not deviate from the path! This makes navigating your work easy for the reader.

3 Signposting body sections

While some lecturers will be fine with you using subheadings in your essay work, this won't always be the case. When you can't use subheadings, you are going to need to use clear signposting to let your reader know when you are done with one topic and are moving on to another one. Doing this well is actually very simple – you just need to use wording that clearly echoes the wording of the introduction you just wrote.

When you are ready to move onto your second topic, for example, you should choose the same words you used in the content overview.

> **Having now provided an overview of** some of the important mythologies of the twentieth century, **I will now position** *Star Wars* within these in order to establish its importance.

As you can see, this sentence both signals that the first topic has been completed and the next one is about to start. You don't always need to do both steps, but if it is at all unclear, then do make sure to remind the reader what they have read already, and show them what will come next.

4 Signposting your conclusion

In our opinion, conclusions are the simplest part of your essay to write, as long as you concentrate on ticking off the 'moves' in Chapter 3 (see Worksheet 5).

When starting your conclusion, there is nothing wrong with really hitting the reader over the head with that fact. Begin with a phrase that clearly signals you are ending your work, something like:

> In conclusion …

> To conclude …

> In sum …

Next, work through the list of content you signposted in the introduction. It is likely that you will use very similar language here; it's okay if it sounds a bit repetitive. Then restate your argument and show that this position is a consequence of the points you discussed in your body paragraphs. In an essay describing experimental research you should also state the limitations here. Finally, explain how your specific position relates to the bigger picture.

5.4 WHAT PASSIVE VOICE IS (AND ISN'T)

Students are often told to 'avoid using passive voice', but we often see manuscripts where lecturers have encouraged people to use it by 'correcting' the grammar. Is the passive voice okay or not?

In English, we are able to construct sentences in both an 'active' voice and 'passive' voice, and these give us options about how we use the *subject* and *object* in a sentence. Remember that an English language sentence has a subject and a verb? (See Section 5.2.) But a sentence also has *objects*. In other words, we have a doer (subject), a thing that they are doing (verb), and a thing that they are doing it to (object). For example:

> **The scientist (subject)** dropped (verb) the pen (object) on the table.

Here, the scientist is the subject (doer), what she is doing (the verb) is dropping, and the object being acted on is the pen. In this sentence, 'on the table' is extra information. This sentence is in active voice, where the subject is explicitly stated.

The alternative is the 'passive' voice:

> The pen was dropped onto the table.

Here, you can see that there is an object (pen) and an action (dropping), but who did the dropping? The doer – the subject – has been left out. If you could add on a doer at the end of a sentence, using the form 'by (person)', then you know it was a passive-voice sentence:

> The pen was dropped onto the table **by the scientist**.

If you have trouble working out if you are writing in the passive voice, you can try this trick developed by Rebecca Johnson … just add 'by zombies' to the sentence. If the sentence makes sense with the 'by zombies' at the end, it is passive – easy!

> After a wand-involved incident, the unicorn body was discovered early on Tuesday morning in a subterranean basement **by zombies**.

> In spite of the greater efforts of the United Council of Vampires, it was not considered possible for the Statutes of 1469 to be amended **by zombies**.

Generally speaking, in an essay it is preferable to use the active voice so that it is clear who said or did the thing that you are referring to, for example:

> Zombies were responsible for a wand-involved incident.

Try reading that last sentence aloud with 'by zombies' at the end – it will sound wrong. Using active voice makes it easier for the reader to identify the actors in your work – and, as we explained earlier, anything that makes your reader's work easier is a good thing.

The passive voice is often a little bit more wordy too, so active voice can help you stay under the word limit. Over a whole essay, a few words here and there really add up!

The active voice is often more straightforward too. If your writing feels convoluted, it may be the fault of the passive voice:

The alcohol was altered by the reaction with the reagent.

vs

The reagent reacted with the alcohol.

You might have been taught to write in the passive voice; some ESL students are taught this way exclusively. Some people use the passive voice to avoid inserting the personal pronoun ('I') into a sentence, for example: 'In this essay, it will be argued that …' But this can also be achieved with the active voice: 'This essay will argue …'

However, there are times where the passive voice is the better choice. If the doer in the sentence is unknown, unimportant or interchangeable, then passive voice is the correct choice. For example, writing something like 'Stone tools were invented before written history' would be just fine – after all, we don't actually know the name of the people who invented them! So most academic writing will use a mix of passive and active voice.

> The term 'passive voice' can be confusing because people sometimes use it, incorrectly, to mean 'any vague and indirect way of writing'. If you receive feedback about 'passive voice' on your writing, what your marker may mean is 'Don't be obfuscatory or unnecessarily vague'. This is really good advice, though it won't necessarily be fixed by inserting the subject back into your sentence!

5.5 HEDGING: HOW TO SAY 'I DON'T KNOW' AND STILL SOUND LIKE YOU DO

Don't make the mistake of thinking a sweeping statement makes your argument 'stronger' because you sound more certain about what you are saying, or because you are making a 'bigger' claim, for example:

> Unicorn hair dissolved in water **always cures** the common cold.

Good academic writing should sound at least a little bit uncertain; it's important that academic knowledge is always open to critique and refinement.

> **Studies suggest that** unicorn hair dissolved in water **may reduce the duration of symptoms** of the common cold.

This book was written during the 2020 COVID-19 pandemic. Some people encouraged others to use drugs that showed promise in trials, but had not gone through all the safety checks yet. As a result, some people died. There is no better example of the danger of overstating the state of knowledge on a topic!

Academic writers are very aware of the dangers of overstating. Part of the way academics avoid overstating is to use 'hedging language': words and phrases that limit the extent of their knowledge claims. Generally, you need to avoid writing in a way that implies your findings and ideas are true, for ever and ever. For example, a scientist who writes a sentence like the following leaves themselves open to critical attack:

Unicorn hair dissolved in water is an effective cure for the common cold.

An unfriendly reader will be asking all kinds of difficult questions, such as: how do you know this for sure? Have you tested enough people? Does it really work for every person ever, or do gender, age or ethnicity make a difference?

If the writer wants to avoid this criticism they would just add:

It's possible that unicorn hair dissolved in water is an effective remedy for the common cold.

Or, if they were more certain:

It's highly likely that unicorn hair dissolved in water is an effective remedy for the common cold.

Or they might retreat behind theory as a shield:

We can hypothesise that unicorn hair dissolved in water is an effective remedy for the common cold.

In the list below we have included phrases that you can use to create protective hedges around the ideas and facts you are not entirely sure about, or where the research has not yet come to a conclusive proof one way or the other:

We can speculate/guess/consider …

Maybe one explanation for this effect is …

With further research we may find that …

This result should be able to be repeated with …

… was an attempt to …

It appears that …

The text suggests / implies …

We should consider the effect of …

We could assume this result means … However …

I propose that …

This result implies …

I intended to …

It is possible that …

The results make us consider whether …

We could predict that …

In one sense …

IN SUMMARY ...

* When you edit your words, focus on how they explain your argument and your ideas, and how your writing conforms to the conventions of academic expression or style.

* Writing clear sentences helps the reader to understand what you are trying to say.

* Signposting language helps a reader navigate your essay.

* Academic writing is often produced to a very tight word count, so knowing how to structure sentences to use fewer words can be helpful.

* Use 'hedging' terms to discuss information that hasn't been categorically proven.

6

WRITING IN ACADEMIC ENGLISH

'Academic English' is a challenge to students who speak English as their first language, as well as students who have learned English as a second or further language. (For simplicity, we'll say 'English as a second language' or 'ESL', as this is the term you often use to describe yourselves to us.) Even if you have spoken and written in standard English all your life, it can be a struggle to translate thoughts into orderly academic prose. That effort is going to be even more challenging if you haven't been writing and speaking English all the way through school. Or perhaps your experience of 'speaking and writing' English has not been 'standard', whether due to speaking another variety of English at home, being neurodivergent, or having a hearing, sight or speaking impairment.

Language barriers can affect grades in essay writing, though not always in the ways you might expect:

- If you were taught in an English-speaking school and uni, you may never have formally been taught grammar or academic style.
- If your first language is not English, there may be challenges in using the grammar you were taught.
- If you are an international student, you might have been taught how to use an academic English style that isn't the same as the style used in your current university.

First, we are going to talk about things that are specific to students who find getting words down in standard English a challenge. Then we offer advice for making the next step into formal academic English.

6.1   WRITING IN ENGLISH

Writing in English can be tough – but you can definitely succeed!

Students are often anxious about their language construction and grammar because that's what they get the most feedback about. This feedback can be misleading. Your lecturers are subject-matter experts, not language teachers. Language advice from lecturers can be a bit hard to interpret and can be misleading. Most English speakers aren't taught technical grammar. It's likely your lecturers learned to write in an intuitive way. They know when something is correct or not, but do not always know why. Seek advice from your writing centre; they should have the right expertise.

Most ESL students have been formally taught grammar, but usually in a way that will help them pass one of the major language tests. Remembering all the rules can be challenging. There are also differences between the way you might use language in a general proficiency test and the way you should use it in a specific discipline's research essay. So we have advice here to help you.

You may also find this advice useful if your first language is sign language, or if you have a sight, speaking or hearing impairment, dyslexia, autism or any other reason that impacts how you experience language and sequences. Where our advice for putting this knowledge into practice suggests 'reading', 'listening' and 'speaking', you should swap in strategies that will work better for you. For example, when we suggest 'reading' articles and highlighting the verbs in different colours, you could use any strategy to identify and count the patterns across sections (for example, by listening to the article, and making a mark in different columns). Your writing centre will be able to work with you to identify strategies for your specific strengths.

Here are some common challenges people encounter when writing essays in English for the first time.

1   Grammar issues

Many lecturers think ESL students struggle most with grammar. We don't agree.

> While you might have a few grammatical errors in your writing, this is unlikely to be the main reason you aren't getting good grades. Fixing those errors won't hurt, but you should prioritise having a clear and well-evidenced argument over totally correct grammar.

Sometimes a grammar issue makes it impossible to understand what you are trying to say, but grammar errors don't often get in the way of understanding your ideas. In fact, many markers are so accustomed to seeing the basic grammar problems they may not even bother to correct them.

Concentrate on having a strong argument, and organising your writing in a structure the reader can follow. State your argument clearly at the beginning of the essay and use clear signposting. This will mean that your lecturer will be able to see what you are trying to say, even if the grammar is not totally accurate.

2   Local academic conventions

Sometimes students are told they have 'grammar problems', but the real problem is that their writing doesn't match the academic style the lecturer expected to read: it 'sounds foreign' or 'sounds wrong'. The grammar itself might have minor issues, but the main issue is that you are not writing according to the relevant academic conventions.

Take some time to read the academic articles on your reading list. Circle any conventions you notice, like whether they use passive or active voice, or any specific vocabulary or phrases. Start to incorporate these conventions into your own writing.

3   What your language leaves out vs what English includes

First ask yourself: where does your language do things differently from English? Why do you think your language does this?

One way to analyse your mother tongue is to write a very direct translation of a sentence in your language into English. Translate the words, not the meaning of the sentence. It's helpful to look at the differences between this sentence and how it should appear in English.

For example:

Japanese: Ringo o tabemashita. Ringo ga akai deshita.

Direct-to-English translation: Apple to ate. Apple [marker] red was.

The Japanese sentence has no subject, so in English, it's not clear who is doing the eating. There is no article so it's not clear how many apples there are. It's not clear if the red apple in the second sentence is the same apple as the one eaten in the first sentence.

Sometimes students will experience 'interference' between their mother tongue and English, with grammatical constructions from the original language slipping into written English. Lecturers are quite used to seeing this kind of 'interference' and can usually work out what you meant to say, but working to eliminate interference will improve your written expression.

Write a list of the common differences between English and your mother tongue. Stick the list up near your computer to remind yourself about what parts of English are most likely to cause you problems.

Neurodiverse students can also benefit from this strategy. Think about what your brain thinks is obvious but other people don't always get. Again, make a list and put it somewhere you will be easily able to refer to it when you are checking over your essays.

4   Direct translation problems

Beware of relying on direct translation and then trying to 'fix' the result. Direct translation, as shown above, can result in quite awkward writing. If you use software like Google Translate, you'll notice it almost always results in unusual language constructions.

Many students tell us from their experience that direct translation is slower, and more frustrating, than trying to write in English in the first place. Persisting in English for all your drafts will help you learn.

You might try talking through your ideas out loud in English, to 'hear' the idea and play around with it, before you try to write it down. Many people find writing in a foreign language much harder than speaking in a foreign language, so start with the easier strategy.

5   Tense use

The tense construction system in English relies on a fairly complex and inconsistent set of verb conjugations rather than time markers. This means that the well-intentioned advice you are given can be confusing, or not quite specific enough.

For example, you may have been told 'you need to always write in the present tense'. This advice usually means the person is asking you to write in the 'present simple' tense, the most common tense in academic writing:

Unicorns **are** not simply horses with an extra horn.

The novel **presents** a narrative of unicorn hunting that **contrasts** significantly with the depiction in the film adaptation.

You may also have been told that introductions are written in the future tense and conclusions in the past tense, and these are definitely the most common tense types you will use in those sections. However, it can be more complicated. For example you might need to use more than one tense in a single sentence:

This essay **will argue (future)** that unicorns **are (present)** not simply horses with an extra horn as **was believed (past)** in the medieval period.

Again, go through an academic article from your reading list or that you are using in your

73

essay. Highlight the verbs using a different coloured pen for future, present and past tenses. What patterns do you see? Is the pattern similar across the whole article, or do you see differences between sections?

6 Article errors

Many languages do not use 'articles' like 'a/ an' and 'the', or they use them differently from English. An English speaker who doesn't know how many of any particular noun is being used will be a little bit uncertain about what you are trying to say.

For example, you could write:

- *an apple*, meaning one of any apple
- *the apple*, one particular apple
- *the apples*, multiple particular apples
- *apples*, any number of any apples.

But if you just write 'apple', an English speaker doesn't know how to interpret that.

The good news with article errors is that their effect on meaning is relatively minor. If you have a list of things you are working on fixing about your English, you should probably concentrate on articles last.

7 Using English every day

If you are an ESL student, you might assume that studying and living in an English-speaking country will mean you will naturally have lots of chances to practise your language skills. But many students find their language skills have not improved, or have even gone backwards, because they aren't using English every day.

Here are some ideas to get you more familiar with English:

- Watch movies or TV shows in English – and try to do it without the subtitles on. This is probably the most relaxing way to learn English! You can pick up a lot of cultural cues as well. Speaking and writing are intimately connected, and fluency in one crosses over to the other.
- Make friends who speak English. Even if most of your friends or housemates share a language other than English, reach out to make connections with local English speakers. Most universities will offer conversational English sessions. There are many student organisations on campus that give you a chance to join in and make new friends through shared activities and interests.
- Find work that requires you to speak English. There's no doubt this will put you in many stressful situations at first, but it will force you to interact with many different types of spoken English and accents. Work is also a good way to make friends with English speakers.
- For any native English speakers who have read this section: you can also help ESL students by chatting with them after class, or inviting them to join your clubs and activities. It's a great way to make new friends yourself.

6.2 IMPROVING YOUR ACADEMIC ENGLISH

This section is relevant for anyone who has been told, or feels, that their academic English has issues. Beyond the basic advice given here, we recommend searching out your university's writing centre, which is often where you will find trained TESOL (Teaching English as a Second or Other Language) staff, alongside specialists in academic writing and learning skills. There are also some excellent books on the subject, including *Academic Writing for International Students* by Siew Hean Read, and Stella Cottrell's *The Study Skills Handbook*.

Spelling and grammar

> Everyone makes small errors of spelling and grammar from time to time. Many markers will not notice, or not think them important enough to point out. But some markers get really obsessed with these problems and will give you feedback that is almost exclusively corrections to spelling and grammar.

A few universities allow the use of a paid copy editor, and some are open minded about getting a friend or a parent to check your grammar. However, other universities call this collusion, so it's probably safer to stick with software if you aren't sure.

Minimising errors is a good idea. Do your best, but don't waste too much energy on perfection.

Apostrophe catastrophes

Apostrophes can be confusing and are often used incorrectly. You are likely to see apostrophe errors regularly in signs, on the internet, and in other non-academic settings, so it's important to understand how to use them correctly in an essay.

You need an apostrophe:

- when you leave out a letter or letters, e.g. *Will you ha' the truth on't?* (Shakespeare, *Hamlet*). You should not use informal

contractions, like *shouldn't*, in formal academic writing.

- to indicate the possessive case, e.g. *Inger's coffee* (thing belonging to a person), *the unicorns' horns* (where the noun is plural). *The walrus' hat* and *the walrus's hat* (where the noun ends in an *s*) are both correct: choose the form recommended in your academic style guide.

You don't need an apostrophe for the possessive of *it*, which is *its*. *It's*, with an apostrophe, is only used as a contraction of *it is*.

Apostrophes can also be used to improve readability of text, for example to form plurals in lowercase words which are not usually plurals (e.g. *do's and don'ts*, *p's and q's*). They are not used for plurals of uppercase letters (e.g. *CVs*), or for years (e.g. *1920s*).

Preposition use

English has a greater number of prepositions than many languages (words like 'for', 'in', 'over', 'through'). Prepositions explain positions in space, the sequence of events in time, or a relationship between things in a sentence. Many people find it difficult to know which preposition to use because English speakers made up all sorts of rules as they went along. Consequently, prepositions can be confusing, even for people who have spoken and written English their whole life.

For example, this sentence is correct:

Translate this poem **into** English **from** Elvish.

But if you change the word order just slightly, you might have to change the prepositions, even if the sentence means exactly the same thing!

Translate **into** English this poem **in** Elvish.

Frustrating! We wish we could give you a set of rules to follow, but there aren't any. The best way to learn to use prepositions correctly is by reading a lot of academic texts. You can also look for exercises online that explain which prepositions go with which words. Try searching for 'collocation' resources.

> These other kinds of English are *not* wrong: they are just suitable for specific contexts. Academic English belongs in essays, academic articles and research presentations – and it would sound very wrong if you used it to write an email to a friend, or to talk to the salesperson at the shops.

Reading academic writing

One of the best ways to improve your grammar is simply to read academic writing. The more you expose yourself to university-level English-language writing, the more you will begin to get used to common patterns in written academic English. In many ways this approach is even better than learning rules from grammar books.

6.3 ADVICE ON 'ENGLISHES' FOR ALL STUDENTS

There are different kinds of English. Using the 'wrong kind' of English in an essay is often more problematic than using the right kind of English with a few grammar errors. If you have ever been told your writing is 'too colloquial', 'too informal' or even 'too flowery', then it's likely you were not using academic English.

Spoken English

If you are told your language is too 'low', 'colloquial' or 'informal', the issue is often that you write like you speak. For example, in spoken English we often contract words (e.g. 'They did not' becomes 'They didn't'), but contractions are rare – or non-existent – in formal academic writing. Moreover, certain kinds of spoken English are closer to academic

written English than others, with some versions of spoken English being considered 'standard' and others considered a 'dialect'.

Modern English is a layered language that draws words from two main sources: Germanic languages and Latin. For centuries, universities taught in Latin, so Latin words are associated with being 'academic', while local languages like English were considered to belong to the uneducated. Even today, some slang or informal words, in what we call a 'non-academic register', have a Germanic origin.

For example, in everyday speech we might say 'shit' or 'poo' (Germanic-origin words), but in an essay, you would probably choose the word 'faeces', or 'defecation' or 'excrement', which are all Latinate terms. You'll notice that the Latinate terms have more syllables – they certainly sound 'fancy', don't they? That's deliberate: academic language developed in monasteries and government offices from the 12th century onwards and is therefore made by 'elites', not the 'commoners'.

If you want to check a word's origin, type 'define' and the word you want to use into Google and look at the origin information. If the word has a German, Dutch, Middle English or Scandinavian origin, you can look at the 'Similar' words, and pick an equivalent that has a Latin or French origin instead. But do check that the new word means exactly the same thing, or you can introduce errors and confusion. We encourage you to use an online dictionary and not an online thesaurus: looking the word up helps you expand your vocabulary and ensure you get the exact match.

One of the areas where we see this the most frequently is in *phrasal verbs*: phrases that indicate action. Here's a list of colloquial phrasal verbs and some more Latinate phrases so you can start to 'get a feel' for (or, we could say, 'comprehend') the switch in tone:

Colloquial		Latinate
blow up	➲	explode
break into the house	➲	force entry to the property
ask around	➲	inquire
get a feel for	➲	comprehend
call on	➲	request
calm down	➲	relax
check it out	➲	investigate

We think you 'get the picture' of the point we are trying to make. But don't get too caught up in where a word comes from. It would also be appropriate to write in an academic essay that you 'understand' – a word that comes from the Germanic!

Literary English

Literary writing is the type of writing you find in serious novels or poems, the kind that you study in English class. It is designed to be read for enjoyment and as an art form.

Literary English uses lots of adjectives (describing words), symbols and analogies to paint a vivid mental picture of people, places

and events. Literature will often omit details or leave things to the reader to imagine for themselves. This is part of the pleasure and purpose of literary writing. Some literature will use long, elegant sentences full of beautiful words as part of its art form.

Students from countries like India, Iran and Italy are taught to write in this more literary way, as are students who studied high school English in Australia. If this is your situation, you don't need to 'improve' your English to write in an academic way because it is already excellent; but you do need to adjust it.

As we've said, probably too often by now, academic English writing in Western countries is designed to convey an argument and give evidence for that argument. Academic English uses only very technical and specific terms to describe things; it tries to avoid ambiguity, and it uses the most straightforward and compact format of sentence it can.

In academic writing, your reader should not have to try to make sense of your argument. Explain all of your ideas in full, and don't leave things out.

Online English

If you have previously read and written English on social media or online platforms, you'll know that academic writing is a big shift. In academic writing, the requirements relating to spelling, punctuation, capitalisation, syntax and form are much less relaxed.

If you have mostly written business English in emails and for web pages, then you will have been trained to avoid long sentences and paragraphs, and to use bullet-point lists or a short synopsis instead.

Academic writing requires full sentences, structured into paragraphs. The tone and language is formal, and it is expected that you will make an effort to proofread before handing it in.

As with all of these examples, the best way to get better at academic writing is to read academic texts, use the feedback from your lecturers and writing centre, and keep practising your essays.

Improving your own skills

Be careful about 'buying in' help. There are many 'essay mills' and services that can sell you essays, but these are illegal in many areas, and heavily penalised in all universities.

Moreover, getting someone else to do your work for you deprives you of the whole point of university: the chance to develop your skills and learn new things. For instance, Grammarly can help you identify issues and rectify them, but try to learn from what the software identifies and changes rather than relying on it to 'fix' your writing.

Learning to write at a more advanced level is challenging for everyone, and giving writing a go, taking on feedback from your lecturers and writing centre, and using resources like this book will help you to learn and improve.

IN SUMMARY ...

* Academic writing has many complex, even hidden conventions that you will need to learn along with the content of your course.

* Both native and non-native speakers of English can experience 'interference' between the kind of language they speak and their written English.

* Do work on your grammar, vocabulary and spelling, but focus more on the argument and evidence in your essay.

7

FINISHING STRONGLY WITH EDITING

You are expected to learn how to edit your own writing at university. It's an important step, so leave at least a little bit of time to read over and correct your writing. You may also need to use editing techniques to get your writing back under the word count, make sure your introduction and conclusion match, include your sources and format the essay.

Lecturers are trained to be pernickety and annoyingly detail-focused. Research has shown that poor grammar or untidy formatting can affect your grades, and leaving out sources or forgetting to put in quotation marks can also lead to marking troubles. In this age of machine-assisted tools, there is less excuse than ever for not getting everything right.

This is really one of the easiest parts of the rubric to tick off, so do it! In this chapter we provide you with tactics for editing.

> It can be tempting to stop working as soon as you have written enough words, in grammatically correct sentences, with your argument stated and an introduction and conclusion.
>
> Especially if you are working right up to the deadline, it can be hard to leave enough time to read through your draft one more time, take a note of any outstanding issues, and also have the time to fix them. But editing really does make all the difference.

If you can take a break before sitting down to edit, we strongly recommend it. If you haven't taken a break, it's harder to see the difference between what is on the page and what was in your head.

Another way to catch errors is to always read the essay aloud at least once before you submit it. It works every time. Inger likes to read her own words out and feel how she is breathing to judge proper sentence length, while Katherine likes to get the computer voice to read it to her. Figure out what works for you!

Ideally, you should schedule at least three to four hours for editing, whether that's all in one block right at the end or broken up into little bits while you write. If you don't have that time, then start with the most important things and work down the list.

7.1 SETTING PRIORITIES FOR EDITING

If you have written a first draft, it can be challenging to know where to start to make it better. Do you start worrying about spelling? What about font and line spacing? Do you start with the introduction or the bibliography?

All of these things are important to get right before you hand in your essay, but some things have a bigger impact on your grades than others, and some things are more effective if they are done in a particular order.

> Even if you feel like 'everything' is wrong with your writing, you won't have time to fix 'everything'. You need to prioritise.

Let's start with fixing the problems that will automatically lead to a poor grade.

1   **Sources**. Check you have properly attributed every quote or paraphrase in the essay. Plagiarism is very serious and can mean an automatic fail, a disciplinary meeting or having to resubmit the work. You might not have it in the totally correct style yet, but make sure you definitely have quotation marks where they need to be, and the author and source are identified.

2   **Word length**. How close are you to the word count? If you write significantly more or less than the word count you are unlikely to get a good grade. Some markers will stop reading when they get to the required word length, so if you are too much over, you have effectively failed to have a conclusion! (See Section 7.2 for ideas on slashing your word count.). If you are massively under the word count, then you probably haven't answered the question in enough depth. Many universities allow you to be 10 per cent above or below the limit but you will need to check.

3   **Argument**. Is your draft logically structured? Does it include relevant material? As we've said again and again in this book, having a strong argument is essential to getting a good grade. If it's rambling or incoherent, or has lots of irrelevant but interesting material, that problem definitely needs to be fixed first.

4   **Due date and time**. Now check how long you have left before you have to hand the work in. Handing work in late may lead to an automatic grade cut in many universities. The first editing steps can take a few hours – especially if you have had to write a lot more material or cut a lot of material out!

Next, you want to work on things that will improve your overall chances of writing an essay your lecturer will love.

1   Do you have a clear introduction and great conclusion? See Chapter 3 for a reminder of what these look like.

2   Have you signposted through the whole essay? See Chapter 5.

3   Use our final checklist (Section 7.3) to polish the writing to a high sheen.

4   Do you have any extra time? Pick something else from this book and level up in that area.

7.2   HOW TO SLASH WORDS WITHOUT TRASHING YOUR WORK

Often an essay will have a recommended length. In many universities, this is set as a 'word count', which is the main way we have discussed it through this book.

If you are significantly over the recommended length, you will need to cut down the number of words in your essay. If you write in a verbose or 'baggy' style, cutting down words will give you room to fit in more of the content that might get you good marks.

Cutting words can be difficult, anxiety-provoking work. The lingering fear of losing some nifty turn of phrase or important detail can get in the way of making a clear and persuasive argument. Part of the skill of writing is to be comfortable with generating and then pruning excess words.

Here are a couple of ideas for cutting an essay back to size. Start with the big picture of whole sentences, then move down to words.

1   Assessing sentences

Start with identifying anything that could be cut. This step involves using the strikethrough tool. That's the option on the top menu of MS Word that ~~does this neat thing~~. The strikethrough function enables you to keep the original text for reference as you rework your text.

Get out the essay question again, and keep it next to you. Then read your essay paragraph by paragraph, referring back to the question constantly. Strike through any sentences that appear to be wandering off the topic, and anything that doesn't really fit, is repetitive or is unimportant.

2   Moving sentences

Not ready to fully delete those sentences yet? Move the sentences you have crossed out with the strikethrough tool to a comment box or footnote. Putting the sentences in footnotes is a good way to hold them 'in reserve'. Leave the sentences at the bottom or side of the page.

One by one, read each paragraph without the removed sentences. Does the paragraph sound better now? Do you need to do some minor repair work to preserve the flow of the text? Only bring a sentence back if you really need it.

3   Deleting sentences

Now look at the sentences still left in the comments or footnotes and reassess. Can you live without them? Yes? We thought so.

Having sorted out the sentences, it's time to get down to individual words.

4   Eliminating filler words

When we speak, we use a lot of 'filler' words, like 'um' and 'ah'. In speech, these words are useful – they give space for you to do some thinking, and for your listener to do some thinking too.

When we are writing our first drafts, extra filler words can give us space to keep typing while thinking, or they can be habits that we fall into without conscious thought while we focus on other, more complex parts of our writing jobs. These words are called *pleonasms*: excess or redundant words.

Removing filler words from your drafts can help with clarity, and with keeping to the word count. Many undergraduate essays are very short: 800–1000 words in some cases. You want to make sure you are using every word you have available to explain your ideas and include relevant information, not take up the space with filler.

> It's easier to preserve the original meaning of the text as you edit if you use a technique like the strikethrough tool or brackets. Keeping all the draft text in view helps you to remember what you were originally trying to say as you rewrite it.

William Zinsser recommends using brackets around words that don't really need to be there, identifying what could be cut first, and later deleting it. For example:

All writers (will have to) edit their prose, but (the) great writers edit (it) viciously, always trying to eliminate (words which are) 'fuzz' – (excess) words (which are not adding anything of value). Zinsser compares (the process of editing out) 'fuzz' to fighting weeds – you will always be slightly behind (because they creep in when you aren't looking for them). Scan (through) your text (and look) for opportunities to (get rid of) words – (places) where two words (can become one), or three words (can become) two … (or where you can get rid of some words altogether.)

Write the paragraph again with the extraneous words removed, and the sentences re-edited slightly to preserve the meaning, to say the same thing in about half as many words.

> All writers edit their prose, but great writers edit viciously. The point of editing is to eliminate 'fuzz', or excess words which don't add value. Zinsser compares removing 'fuzz' to fighting weeds, because you will always be slightly behind. Scan your text for opportunities to shed words: where can two words become one? Or three words two?

'Filler word' checklist

Here is a quick checklist for filler words that you can delete or replace with shorter alternatives.

1   Delete long introductory phrases like '**In order to understand this phenomenon we must** first assess' or 'As Lee **makes clear**'. Replace with a crisper phrase like 'First I will assess' or 'Lee demonstrates'.
2   Delete tautologies, or repeated phrases like '**final** conclusions' or '**initial** introductions'. We know conclusions are final and introductions are initial, so replace with 'conclusions' or 'introductions'.
3   Delete 'the idea of' words. When we are thinking about things, we can focus

on the thinking, rather than the thing. This can lead to phrases like '**The conceptualisation of the idea of** global markets', which can probably be shortened to something like 'Global markets'.

4   Replace the filler words with meaningful words. Excessive use of pronouns (words like 'it', 'which' and 'they'), demonstratives (like 'this' and 'that') and prepositions (like 'throughout', 'between' and 'among') can produce unclear writing. What does 'that' refer to? What does 'it' refer to? Explain every time. This strategy can sometimes increase the number of words you use, but they are all valuable words!

5   In other cases, excessive pronouns, demonstratives and prepositions show that you could rewrite the sentence to be much shorter. For example: 'It was demonstrated **that throughout** history, **they** were **among** the most important thinkers in their field' can be rewritten as 'Freud and Klein are important thinkers in the field of psychology'. Rewriting not only cut out lots of extra words, but gives the reader much clearer, more precise and more accurate information.

6   Reduce adjectives and adverbs (describing words). This is also a good strategy if you are using lots of words like 'fast', 'good' or 'importantly'. Replace these with data or more concrete information like 'at 100 km/hr', 'achieved the stated goal' or 'won the Nobel Prize'.

7   Sometimes, no matter how much you delete or replace individual words, the whole paragraph seems vague. This is the time to step back from the detail of your writing and ask, 'What do I really need in order to prove my argument?' One very strong example or piece of evidence is more effective than lots of circumstantial clues. So explain the most important

information and give your strongest piece of evidence. And then move on!

A major source of filler words are verbs. Helen Sword in *The Writer's Diet* suggests replacing verbs like 'have, do, show', and limiting your use of 'be-verbs' (is, am, are, was, were, be, being, been).

Consider this sentence, which is loaded with verb forms of 'to be':

> Unicorns **are** magical creatures which **are** to **be** found in the most remote, inaccessible parts of the Australian rainforest, where they **have been** living in peace for centuries. (28 words)

If we rewrite the sentence with no 'to be' verbs, it is half the length while still saying essentially the same thing:

> Magical unicorns **have lived** peacefully in remote, inaccessible parts of the Australian rainforest for centuries. (15 words)

7.3   THE FINAL STAGES

Just before you hand your essay in, give it one last read-through. This is the time to double-check everything is ready to go.

1   Make sure the words you used are the ones you meant to use

Begin by turning on the spelling and grammar settings in MS Word, or copy the text into a machine-assisted editor like Grammarly. Consider the software a helper, and also use your own eyes, knowledge and critical judgment. Software is most helpful for spotting basic errors, including word repetition, missing letters and other

typing errors. Remember English has minor differences from country to country: make sure you have the correct dictionary loaded so the spell checker does not create yet more confusion. Software is getting more sophisticated; if you can set a 'tone', dial it all the way up to super formal!

English has many words that look or sound similar but mean completely different things. (Words that have the same pronunciation but different meanings are called *homophones*.) Do a careful read-through to see if you can find any incorrect word usage that the machine might not pick up because the spelling is correct, but you've typed the wrong word. Here is a list of commonly confused words:

lose / loose

effect / affect

allusion / illusion

than / then

bought / brought

there / they're / their

you're / your

elicit / illicit

to / too / two

chose / choose

through / threw / thorough / though

lead / led

practice / practise

WORKSHEET 14 // WORDS YOU GET MIXED UP

Write down words that are a challenge for you, and you often mix up. Use this list next time your write an essay to help you catch them before they slip through to your markers!

Words that I get mixed up all the time are:

_____

_____

_____

_____

_____

_____

_____

_____

_____

_____

_____

_____

_____

_____

_____

_____

_____

_____

_____

_____

_____

_____

Look up the meanings to make sure you know the difference. A good dictionary is still an essential study aid!

2   *Capitalisation and italics*

Capitalising words and using italics create emphasis in text, but both must be handled with care and consistency. Be sparing with capital letters for types of places or people. Do capitalise when you are referring to a specific person or place, e.g. Prime Minister Julia Gillard; Australian National University. But you typically would use 'prime minister' and 'university' for the general thing.

Check the capitalisation rules for titles. Different style guides have different views on which words should have capitals and which shouldn't.

You should not usually use italics for emphasis in an academic essay. Nor would you typically use italics for quotations; instead, most style guides suggest you use quotation marks or a block text style.

Do use italics for titles of books, plays, blogs, newsletters, journals and so on, e.g. *Unicorn Handlers: Histories 1739–1854*; *Journal of Unicorn Management*; *Monthly Unicorn Summary*. Italics are not used to refer to article titles, chapter titles or the names of other sections of text. Instead, use single quotes around plain body text, e.g. 'Theorising unicorn hair for medicinal use in Australian farm management'.

3   *Numbers*

Using numbers in text can be tricky, and lack of attention to handling numbers makes your text look amateurish. There is no hard and fast rule here, but consistency goes a long way to creating the right impression in your reader. Here are some suggestions:

- Usually, spell out numbers in full below ten, and then use digits for 11 onwards. If the number is at the start of a sentence, always spell it in full.
- Always use digits for time or object measurements, e.g. *6:50 am, 51 cm*.
- Always use digits for percentages, e.g. *46% of people* or *56 per cent of people*.
- Write money amounts in digits; you should also include the currency symbol and/or code: e.g. *US$100, GBP300* or *¥200*.

4   *Quotations*

Academic writing uses formatting conventions to help the reader understand what text is yours and what text was authored by others. Conventions vary, so check with your lecturer, but here are some suggestions:

- Use 'single quotation' marks around short pieces of imported text.
- Use "double quotation" marks for a quotation within another quotation, but try not to use these too often.
- If your quote is longer than three lines, indent the text as a block quote. You do not use quotation marks or italics for block quotes. However, as a general rule, avoid using block quotes, especially of secondary literature – your marker might think you have not done enough work to digest the ideas in the text. (See more in Chapter 8 about kinds of evidence.)
- If you do include a block quote, explain the reason for including the quote just before you use it, because eye-tracking experiments suggest that readers tend to skip over indented text.

5 Dashes

Most people do not realise there are different kinds of dashes or hyphens until they reach university. Your keyboard can do hyphens, en dashes and em dashes. Here are some guidelines for use:

- Use an en dash (–) to indicate spans of numbers and dates, e.g. *12–15 times*; *1988–2004*.
- Use an en dash between proper nouns (names of places or people) of equal value, e.g. *New Zealand–Australia relations*. You can also use an en dash between common nouns that are unlikely combinations, e.g. *space–time continuum*.
- Hyphens (-) belong between two words to make them into one concept, e.g. *double-check*.
- Hyphens join a compound adjective when it immediately precedes a noun, e.g. *a well-known phenomenon, a twentieth-century historian*.
- Hyphens can help to avoid ambiguity, particularly for measurements and descriptions, i.e. *twelve-monthly intervals* or *190cm-long unicorn horns*.
- You can use a spaced en dash (–) or an unspaced em dash (—) to mark a sudden break in thought, or to give some information added emphasis. However, this is more often used in informal writing and can be overused in essays. It is often better to replace these dashes with commas, reorder the sentence, or add emphasis in another way.

6 Check formatting and style

Your next job is to look at the formatting of your text to make sure it is consistent. Make your life easy by setting up some basic text styles. First, check the text:

- The standard setting for body text is left-aligned, ragged-right alignment (not fully justified). Use the icon that looks like ▤ .
- Headings, including headings within tables, should be left-aligned and bold.
- Check any lists. Avoid listing the same item twice. Bullet points should be formatted as separate lists and not merged with paragraph text.
- Check all web addresses, anchors and footnotes. Do they link to the right information?

Now check the consistency of your style. If your lecturer has set a particular style guide (like APA or Chicago), then use that style.

- Check your references are in the correct style.
- Choose a format for the various dates, place names or titles in your essay and make sure the format is used consistently.
- Check any captions related to graphics, and any headings attached to graphs, tables and charts.
- Ensure figure numbers are sequential in the text and match any figure numbers you have cross-referenced in your document.
- The final job is to look at your abbreviations and symbols. The first time you use an acronym you must spell out the term in full, e.g. British Broadcasting Corporation (BBC).

7 Hand it in!

Just before you hand in your essay:

- Use your spelling and grammar checker one more time!

- Make sure your essay is in 12-point font, double-spaced, with a 1 inch (2.54 centimetre) margin – or whatever your lecturer requests.
- Put in the page numbers, and your student number or name.

Finally, do whatever you need to do to get your essay to the marker on time. Uploading a document to your learning management system might sound like it will take a few seconds, but when you are tired and rushed you can face unexpected hurdles, like accidentally sending in the wrong draft, or sudden wi-fi dropouts. Give yourself time for things to not quite go to plan at that moment! Inger is still traumatised by the last-minute rush before her PhD thesis submission, when the file became corrupted and she had to do a lot of the work again from a much earlier version. Don't be Inger – keep back-ups.

And then make a note of what you did, how long each step took, and what you'd like to do differently next time.

We often underestimate how long it takes to do certain editing tasks (this book took two months longer than we thought it would and between us we have decades of experience!), so getting a realistic idea will be a massive bonus next time. You can add the suggestions your lecturer makes in the feedback to your list and use them as boosters for your next essay. (See Section 7.5, on page 89, for more on this.)

7.4 COMMON EDITING MISTAKES AND MISSTEPS

Save yourself some hassle and avoid these common editing mistakes.

1 **Rewriting your text to use bigger words, longer sentences and more complex grammar.** Some students think that using polysyllabic vocabulary produces the appearance of greater intelligence. Sometimes academic writing does need big words and longish sentences to put across complex ideas, but simpler writing is often surprisingly more effective.

2 **Not using your judgment when using machine tools** for spelling, grammar, good writing or citations. Don't ignore the red or green scribbly lines in MS Word, but you don't always have to follow the suggestions strictly. Sometimes you will be using language the machine doesn't recognise because it does not have a completely comprehensive dictionary and does not recognise 'jargon' or specialist technical language.

Software like Turnitin works to match text and compare it to other published work and other students' work. Sometimes it will pick up phrases that your whole class have used, like repeating the language of the essay question, a quotation correctly referenced, or a section that is likely to be similar across essays like a methods paragraph. It is important to use your judgement to see if these are signs you are copying someone else's work, or if you are actually answering the question, working with the sources or describing the same experiment, as you are supposed to do!

Similarly, be careful using software with settings to help you with 'tone', like Grammarly. Online tools can help you see where you are not 'engaging' or when you are using the passive voice, but only you can judge if this is an issue. Often it is appropriate for a research essay.

3 **Not taking a break between writing and editing.** When you are too close to your work, you know what you meant to say and can forget that your reader cannot see into

your mind. When you come back to your writing after a good break, you can see all the missing words, garbled sentences and information you have left out.

4 **Refusing to edit your work at all**. Avoiding rewriting your essays means you are letting lots of marks go.

5 **Being a drama queen and deleting everything**. You may need to do some deleting and some rewriting, but most of the time you won't get a better essay by writing a series of first drafts. Work with what you have written and make it better.

6 **Only writing and reading on the screen**. Most people skim-read when they are reading on screens. If you find it hard to see errors on a screen, try reading your essay aloud or printing it out to help you notice the details.

7 **Confusing big-picture editing with finding the small errors**. There are actually two different stages of editing, and you need to do both. You need to look at the question, the rubric and your argument in order to make strategic decisions about what to include, and to find the most logical way to structure your work. This kind of editing is about answering the question strategically. We talked about this in Section 7.1, on setting priorities for editing, because you usually do this first.

In polishing your work, you check spelling, grammar, vocabulary, punctuation and formatting. We tackled this level of editing in the previous section. You might double-check small details like citation styles, or fact-check your claims. (Is it really on page 127? Did that happen in January or February? Was it 81 or 82 per cent?) This kind of editing is about avoiding mistakes. You usually do it after you have decided on the big picture.

8 **Not checking the style guide**. Your style guide is your friend for much more than just how to format citations. It will help you decide how to format headings, when to use 'seven' or '7', whether the passive voice is used and so on. Style guides are used by researchers to edit and format their published works, so you will also sound much more academic if you use the guides.

9 **Ignoring feedback**. Remember that previous essay that you got some comments on? Did you read them? We know many students don't. Actually, that feedback is a goldmine of personalised advice from your lecturer on exactly what you need to do next time to improve your grade. (See Section 7.5 for more.)

10 **Thinking everything is wrong with your writing**. This is a common issue with all students and particularly ESL students. If you make the same errors a lot, it can feel like everything is wrong with your writing. But normally it's just that you have a short list of things you often stuff up, like subject–verb agreement, tense, passive voice, misspelling words, or mixing up words. Make a list, and check off each issue individually. You will always have a list, though what's on it might change as you get more experience!

11 **Not putting the argument and ideas first**. We've banged on about this problem for nearly a whole book now, but one more time is a charm! Essays are less about 'good' writing, and more about strong arguments and interesting ideas. Work on being clear, accurate, logical and focused. The words might not be pretty, but if your thinking is sophisticated and original, then your writing will be academic.

7.5 HOW TO USE FEEDBACK TO IMPROVE YOUR WRITING

Getting feedback is one of the benefits of going to universities to learn rather than just logging into a free online course. Sure, you can write an essay, hand it in and wait for the mark as your 'feedback', or you can get someone to give you constructive feedback along the way.

> Many universities offer support from peer advisors, or writing centres, where you can get feedback before you hand work in. These are extremely useful, and give you an added advantage when trying to level up. Students who are getting the best marks are making use of every resource, including the writing centre.

We also see many degrees and subjects that build up your skills across a series of assignments – perhaps starting with a short annotated bibliography or analysis piece that isn't worth many marks. The point of this assignment is to get some feedback on your writing skills and build you up to a research essay. If you don't read the feedback on the earlier task, you won't get the boost or insider tips for tackling the big essay that can be worth 40–50 per cent of your mark.

If you aren't sure how to put your lecturer's feedback into practice, go along to the lecturer's office hours, or go to see a writing centre advisor. They will be able to unpack what it means and give you strategies to improve.

Everyone finds dealing with constructive criticism hard. When you have put in a lot of work, it would be nice to get a gold star and some in-game diamonds. It's okay to find ways to take on the feedback but also feel good about yourself. For example, some people make sure they have a nice hot drink and something yummy to eat before opening the feedback. Other people have a trusted buddy who will read the feedback and warn them if it's going to be hard to read.

Mostly we find that feedback is least difficult to take on board when it's separated from the finished assignment, and instead used as part of the planning process for the next essay. Since this is the purpose of university feedback, it's not surprising it works best when we use it to feed-forward.

IN SUMMARY ...

* Editing can take longer than you expect! Make sure you leave time between finishing your essay and editing it.

* Try to do your editing in two stages: start with 'the 'big picture' overview of the essay structure, where you are checking for organisation and logic; and then move on to the detailed 'polish', where you are checking for typos and consistency.

* Part of the learning process is to engage with the feedback on your writing. Make use of all the advice and support your university offers you.

PART 3

PLANNING FOR NEXT TIME

As you will have already noticed, as one essay is submitted, the next one is already coming up over the horizon. Calmly producing a good essay, rather than white-knuckling through it at the last minute, is the sign of a truly 'grown-up' writer. The process of achieving Zen-like calm around assignments begins well before you sit down to write. This section is dedicated to helping you become the kind of professional writer who takes each essay in their stride.

If you are reading this book before you start uni, then you can put our suggestions into practice from day one. But you can also use this part of the book to prepare for next time. These final two chapters discuss things that are often at the beginning of books like this – how to take notes, how to read, how to plan your time.

Writing a well-structured, well-researched essay is much easier if you have planned your time and done your research well! As Stephen Covey points out in *The 7 Habits of Highly Effective People*, 'continual improvement' involves taking time to improve our skills and technique, not just jumping in and trying to do the job as quickly as possible. His analogy is useful: take time to sharpen the saw before trying to cut down a tree.

So, let's enhance our equipment, stock up on our health potions and get ready to push on to the next level.

8

RESEARCH AND NOTE-TAKING

In this chapter we introduce you to some of our favourite tips and tricks for compiling evidence, reading and taking notes before you even start writing your essay.

You will need to collect data and evidence to support the main argument in your essay. If you don't, you might get feedback similar to the following real comment on an essay:

> In this paper you have demonstrated that you have understood some of the core elements of the relevant subject matter. However, the main weakness of this paper is that it is not an essay, but rather an opinion piece. An academic essay is (in simple terms) an argument supported by evidence. You have an argument, but your paper is entirely devoid of any evidence. Source: Matthew Jones, University of Greenwich, London

> We have said again and again that an argument is critical to an essay, but an argument without evidence is just an opinion. A research essay is about the *research* you have done. It is different from an opinion piece or a personal reflection.

First, we'll talk about the different kinds of evidence and how they are generally used in research essays. Then we'll talk about how to engage with the evidence through reading, note-taking and quotations.

8.1 DIFFERENT KINDS OF EVIDENCE

All research essays require you to find and use 'evidence'. Knowing what kinds of evidence you are looking for, and how to decide which sources are most relevant, reliable and persuasive, can be challenging. If you have to write both science and humanities essays, you will notice that they consider different kinds of evidence as valid or invalid, and they use them very differently!

Peer-reviewed articles and books are the most common form of evidence acceptable in research essays, but evidence comes in many forms. In Chapter 3, we noted that you should explain any evidence that is not from an academic source. In this section we help you to develop a nuanced understanding of the differences between types of evidence, as well as how and when to use them.

Primary and secondary sources

Here's a quick refresher on the difference between primary and secondary sources of evidence. *Primary* sources give you direct evidence or firsthand testimony. Primary sources can take many forms, such as texts, objects, sound files, ledgers, census records, photographs. Historical artefacts, artworks, literary texts and works of theory are also primary sources.

Primary sources can be reliable, complete and from a highly believable source. For example, a photograph or diary entry of someone who was an eyewitness to an event, backed up by other evidence, is a reliable source. Primary sources can also be unreliable, incomplete or from a less credible source – perhaps the eyewitness was inconsistent in recording dates, or only jotted down a few notes, or has a reason to spin the story.

A *secondary* source is someone else's interpretation of the evidence – whether that's a government report, a newspaper story, a popular book about the topic, or a peer-reviewed article.

Trustworthy and untrustworthy secondary literature

Not all books and articles are the same. Peer-reviewed, scholarly publications are the 'gold standard' for evidence at universities. This means that you can expect that the authors are qualified; they have declared any potential conflicts of interest; their work has been professionally edited; and their work has been read and approved by other academics not involved in the research project. A peer-reviewed paper will include academic evidence, fully referenced.

However, this doesn't mean the published research is always correct, or the only answer. Students often assume that if the evidence is presented in the form of a book or article, it is automatically credible and current. Some books and articles are – but you should check.

Here is a checklist for evaluating how credible and current your secondary sources are.

1   The date of publication

Typically, you want secondary sources from the last five to ten years, although in some disciplines you might go back 20 years. That means anything published in the 20th century is probably not current anymore.

But it can be somewhat more complicated than that. In some science disciplines, work published five years ago might already have been overtaken by more recent publications. On the other hand, in Classics it is totally appropriate to use some of the critical secondary literature first published 2000 years ago (for example, Aristotle interpreting the plays of Sophocles).

It also depends on what you are using the evidence for. An archaeological case report from 40 years ago containing observations about the undisturbed state of a site will be useful in a different way from a more recent article that describes what was dug up last year.

2   The publisher

Some books and articles are published by academic publishers, and have been peer reviewed. This is what is meant by a 'scholarly source'. If it is published by a non-academic publisher, you need to dig deeper to check its publications are reliable for academic work.

For example, there is a lot of so-called 'grey literature' out there: reports containing research findings that may or may not have been subjected to peer review. Grey literature may include reports by government bodies like the Australian Bureau of Statistics, or policy statements by organisations or by researchers. While this kind of grey literature has not been peer reviewed, it *is* produced by credible researchers and backed by a serious research organisation. Other 'grey' sources are more suspect, such as those produced by 'think tanks', lobbying groups, industry-funded publicity companies or marketing firms. Just be aware that grey literature producers can have an agenda that makes it unlikely they will be producing balanced and reliable research.

Whenever you read grey literature, ask yourself: who is writing this piece? Are the people producing the evidence credible? Do they have a hidden agenda? Ask your lecturer about using grey literature if you aren't sure, and always make sure to state that it's a report or policy when using it in your essay.

3 Whether it is connected to the rest of the scholarly secondary literature

Do the authors reference other academic literature, or mostly newspaper articles and things they found on the web? Do other articles reference them? (You can check that in Google Scholar or your library database.)

4 Use of other sources

It is always worth tracking important evidence back to its source. You might find you don't agree with the interpretation you are reading, or you might find they have inaccurately represented the material they reference.

Academic vs personal evidence

When you are writing a research essay, you typically need to use scholarly evidence rather than personal reflection.

The following statement is based on feelings and personal experience.

> I feel that experimenting on unicorns is wrong because when I saw one at the zoo, I got close enough to look into its eyes. The unicorn felt very human to me.

Personal feelings, one person's experiences and anecdotes only tell us about how one person experiences the world. They cannot be used to make general claims about how other people would experience the same thing (or even how the unicorn is experiencing the event).

If you are writing an essay that needs to make objective, scientific, provable or generalisable claims, you will need to look for different kinds of evidence – such as experiments written up in academic journals:

> Experimentation on unicorns is unethical as they have been demonstrated to both understand and fear painful procedures (Gēṇḍā, 2016).

Evidence at different scales

Think about how much you can, or should, generalise from the evidence you have. Some disciplines encourage you to look big for general trends, and other subjects encourage you to stick with the particular case or work you are exploring. Typically, though, you can't make grand claims if you've only looked at a small piece of evidence. For example, an archaeology student using claims from only one dig is unlikely to be able to make claims about other sites, while a student who includes data collected from multiple digs can talk about more sites.

Always think about whether, and to what extent, you can 'scale up' the evidence you are using to make a bigger point. It is worse to overclaim than to be careful and specific.

8.2 HOW TO FIND EVIDENCE

Many universities will run extra sessions alongside your classes, with the writing centre or the library, on how to search for written scholarly evidence. They are very helpful, and always worth attending. We'll touch on some general points here, and then give you one bonus strategy you probably won't get in that session.

Search strategies

In everyday life, if we want to find out about something we'll type our question into Google and see what comes up. We'll click through to a couple of different sites, like Wikipedia and WebMD, and perhaps follow up by asking around our friends and family. This is a good way to get the general gist of a topic, but it doesn't provide the kinds of evidence you need for a research essay.

> Rather than typing your key terms into Google, use Google Scholar. This is the bit of Google that searches for academic texts, though it also brings up reports, reviews and sometimes blog posts. You will be able to connect to the material by being connected to your university wi-fi, or through your library sign-in to get access to journal articles that are behind a 'paywall'. The library will have its own search tool, too. It might give you access to both books and articles, but sometimes there is a separate book catalogue – so check both.

Knowing what to type into the search field can be a challenge. Many people just type in the essay question but this tends to have limited success. Instead, identify search terms from the essay question and your planned argument.

If you are in a discipline that uses books, go to the library and find the section that deals with your broad topic. The books will have been sorted so that you should find related books shelved nearby.

If you have done all of these searches, you will probably have brought up more articles and books that you could ever read. You can then use a strategy like the 'bedraggled daisy diagram' below to narrow down the sources to ones that are more relevant.

Here are some other tips to identify which sources might yield effective evidence.

- Use articles to answer questions that can be best addressed through a single study.
- Use books (e.g. biographies, theories) to answer general questions that take a larger view.
- Use encyclopaedias and dictionaries to look up short definitions.
- Look at the footnotes and bibliographies of the books and articles you were given as set readings. Do they reference any works you have brought up in your massive list?

Bedraggled daisy diagram

Once you have already decided on your topic and approach, you can use a bedraggled daisy diagram to plan a literature review, or to help you search the literature to find relevant evidence for your essay, The bedraggled daisy was first introduced by Kristin Luker in *Salsa Dancing in the Social Sciences*, and it is basically a Venn diagram on steroids. It helps you to identify effective search terms to type into Google Scholar, your library search tool or database, and to narrow down the results if you get too many.

How to make a bedraggled daisy diagram:

1 Brainstorm a list of up to eight potential search terms.
2 Write each of these terms on the petals of the daisy (one term per petal).
3 The overlap between the petals suggests some intersections you might want to explore. You can do this by typing in both search terms and seeing what you get.
4 Type the first search term into your search tool and see if there are any resources. If there are too many, put two search terms in at once, which will narrow down the results.
5 Keep going until you have gone around the daisy and have some really relevant sources for every 'petal'.

We've done a (silly) worked example below:

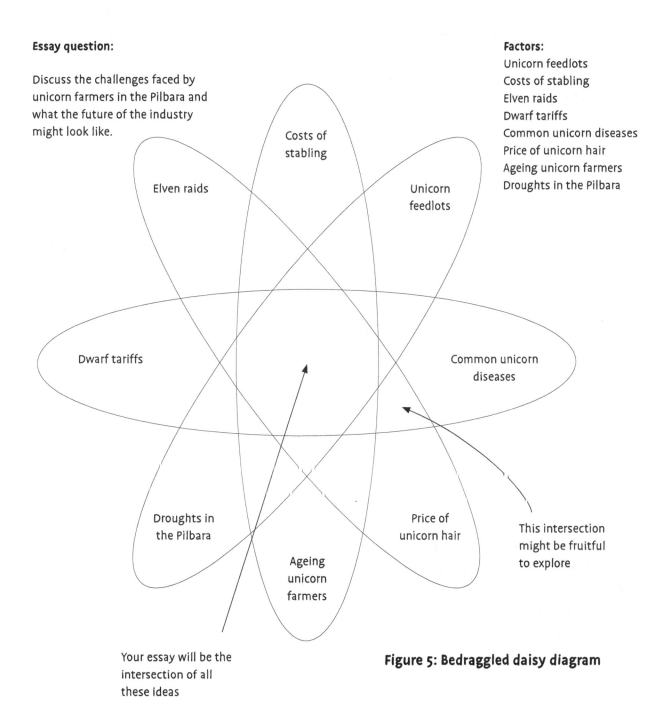

Essay question:

Discuss the challenges faced by unicorn farmers in the Pilbara and what the future of the industry might look like.

Factors:
Unicorn feedlots
Costs of stabling
Elven raids
Dwarf tariffs
Common unicorn diseases
Price of unicorn hair
Ageing unicorn farmers
Droughts in the Pilbara

Costs of stabling

Elven raids

Unicorn feedlots

Dwarf tariffs

Common unicorn diseases

Droughts in the Pilbara

Price of unicorn hair

Ageing unicorn farmers

This intersection might be fruitful to explore

Your essay will be the intersection of all these ideas

Figure 5: Bedraggled daisy diagram

Relevance of the evidence

You can gather a lot of evidence but if it doesn't specifically talk about your essay topic, it's not likely to be relevant. Irrelevant evidence won't be counted for your grade.

Some things to check for relevance:

1 Does the source use the same key words as your essay question or answer?
2 Does it address the same theme or topic?
3 Does it match the period / region / genre / demographic / materials etc. as your essay?
4 Does it use the same theoretical approach as your essay?
5 Does it measure things in the same way as you will be doing in your essay?

You don't need all of these to match, but if none of them are even close then you need to rethink what evidence you are using!

8.3 ACTIVE READING STRATEGIES

Writing a good essay isn't only about writing – it is also about reading. If you are writing a *research* essay, you will need to do quite a lot of reading to satisfy the *research* component.

Undirected reading can be a waste of time. If you haven't given much thought to which parts of the reading to focus on, you might end up reading whole articles, every word, front to back … and then realise they weren't at all relevant to your essay.

Separate the searching-for-material phase and the reading phase. If you get caught up in reading as you are searching, the process takes longer and you are more likely to wander off track. The trick to reading effectively is to always be reading with a specific goal in mind and with a pencil or keyboard within reach.

Here's a step-by-step guide to help your reading be targeted and time-efficient.

1 Start with what you know already

Before you start reading, write down some of the key things that you know already about your essay topic. Some of this you will have picked up from your lectures and tutorials, some from the reading set for the class. This process doesn't take long – just dot points will be fine for now.

2 Think about what you'd like to know more about

Phrase these as actual questions, and write them down.

3 Select the most relevant material that you have found

Using the key words from your questions, pick out the sources that are most likely to be useful to you. Read the titles and subtitles, and the abstracts or blurbs to guess. If you have downloaded the sources as PDFs or ebooks, you can use your computer's search function to see if they use your key words in the body of the text too. Continue with this process until you've gathered up a handful of promising sources.

If any of the articles look as though they aren't going to answer your questions, discard them. Don't fall into the trap of academic FOMO. You can't read everything, because we truly do live in an age of information abundance.

4 Skim-read – it's a legitimate academic strategy!

You have your pile of likely articles – should you now sit down and read through each one? No! One of the best kept secrets at universities is that you don't have to read every word of every paper to reach enough understanding of its content to write.

> In their article 'The active skim', Hannah Wohl and Gary Alan Fine challenge the idea that good students are those who read everything completely. They argue that 'active skimming is not a lazy task' and should be taught as a legitimate skill. The trick is to work out when to skim and when not to skim – save your in-depth reading for a small number of important texts.

So this is the time to do a fast read-through of your pile without taking any notes at this stage. The fast read is just that: fast! Set a timer and see if you can run your eye over the whole thing in five minutes or less. Often, just reading the first 'topic' sentence of each paragraph is sufficient for you to get a grip on the flow of arguments or ideas.

You'll find, as you practise this technique, that you will hone what Wohl and Fine call the skill of 'selective attention'. Your eye will start to pick up themes, concepts or ideas that are useful. Use this process to choose a small number of texts that are clearly relevant for the questions you wrote down earlier in step 2.

5 Deep-read with your guiding questions

Now look at the texts you have chosen while keeping your questions in mind. The act of looking for an answer to your question will help you decide which parts of the articles to read.

For some articles, you might only need to deeply read the introduction; for others, only the discussion, and so on. Deeply read only what you need to answer your question. If you are lucky, the whole article or book will be relevant, but this is not usually the case. As you start to find answers to your initial questions, jot down dot-point answers.

You might then come up with some new and more nuanced questions in order to continue your search. Search more, if you need to – but put limits on your reading or you will be there forever.

6 Respect your limits

Increasing the efficiency and effectiveness of your reading means you can get through more sources and find relevant material relatively easily. But you can't do it mindlessly; the strategy relies on you having enough mental energy to be thinking of questions and trying to find answers to those questions. As a result, our reading strategy works best if you pace yourself.

We generally wouldn't recommend trying to deeply read more than five or six articles in a day. This is where planning matters – as we say in the next chapter, even if you are someone who can write late, you shouldn't be trying to *read* late.

It's even more effective if you get into the habit of reading a few articles a day, starting a couple of weeks before your essay is due. By the time you sit down to write, you should have not only actively read enough articles,

WORKSHEET 15 // WHAT DO YOU ALREADY KNOW?

Write down what you know and the questions that will
guide your reading for your current project.

_____

_____

_____

_____

_____

_____

_____

_____

_____

_____

_____

_____

_____

_____

_____

_____

_____

_____

_____

_____

_____

_____

_____

_____

_____

but you should also have answered enough of your own questions to start to shape these into the essay itself.

8.4 ACTIVE NOTE-TAKING STRATEGIES

Writing exclamation marks or emojis in the margins of a printout, or running a fluorescent pen across a piece of text, are not active note-taking strategies. They can be useful to help you keep paying attention to your reading but if you want to generate useful notes, you will need to actually do some writing.

Knowing what to write down when you are listening to lectures, or when you are reading books and articles full of important information, is one of the big challenges at uni. And once you have written the material down, the next big challenge is often knowing how to use that information in your assignments.

There are many useful ways to take notes, including mind-mapping, outlining and summarising. Use different kinds of note-taking for different kinds of class. For example, in a content-heavy science class, where you have to learn lots of facts for an exam, you could summarise the information into a quiz or cue-cards to test your recall. In a group tutorial, take notes as a to-do list of things you want to look up later. To help you pay attention while reading an article, you might annotate the text with highlighting and make detailed comments in the margins. These are all called 'active' note-taking methods, where your brain engages with the information, and then you take notes that will help you do the learning task that comes next.

We assume you already know to write down quotes, information and ideas you have while reading. The following note-taking strategies enhance your tools to take you to the next level.

Don't copy everything down

The research tells us that the worst way to take notes is to try to write everything down. Not only is copying down everything in a lecture tiring and stressful, it's also uncritical. You can't take the time to understand the information or decide how useful or important it is. When we just copy stuff, we don't remember; we don't understand; we don't make connections; we write down things that are fundamental next to things that are incidental.

Simply transcribing what a lecturer is saying means that the lecturer's voice will probably go onto the page without going through our brains. It's even worse if you are copying and pasting text from your readings to your essay document. It's easy to dump whole sentences and paragraphs in your notes without taking the time to decide which words or phrases are most useful. You don't engage your brain to summarise or judge the work. And it's far too easy to get confused about what you have written yourself, and then run into issues about being insufficiently original, which we talk more about in the next section.

These days most lectures and resources are available as recordings, slideshows or full text. Books and articles are available online, so you can borrow them again, or store them on your own computer. If you missed something, you can easily go back and find it again.

Just like reading, note-taking is most productive if you do it with a purpose. Since your current purpose is to write an essay, the first step is to think about how much information from each source can be included in the essay. You don't have many words, so one short quote or a few facts is all you will be able to include. Don't write down everything, just the relevant information.

Here are some things to consider when you are trying to choose what information to include.

- For most research essays, you would be expected to quote or paraphrase only a few words or phrases from any one source.
- Most research essays want you to synthesise (that is, draw information together from multiple sources), not to paraphrase extensively from a single source.
- Most arts and humanities subjects expect you to use minimal information from lectures. Other subjects or kinds of essays may have different rules, so ask your lecturer if you are unsure.

If you can only include a few phrases or a short paraphrase, your notes should be a place to select the most effective information to include. Think about why the information is relevant. Every note you take should have a purpose:

- Does it help build your argument?
- Does it explain a term you are using?
- Does it provide evidence for a claim you are making?

In note-taking, you should also include your own thoughts and reactions. These thoughts are most useful when they are about critiquing the source you are reading, making connections with other sources, or bringing multiple sources together to produce new insights. This is what lecturers mean when they say 'synthesis'.

Use your notes to reduce plagiarism risks

University work needs to be a balance of relying on the research and writing of other people, and producing your own insights into the topic. It's easy to accidentally claim someone else's work as your own if you have not been careful about how you take notes – for example, by dumping large copied-and-pasted segments into your Word document and then writing over them.

> If you get really muddled, you may present work you copied as part of your essay, and that is plagiarism. However, it's easy to avoid inadvertent plagiarism if you are careful about referencing the sources you have used, keep good notes about what you read separate to your planning document, and understand the difference between *quoting*, *paraphrasing* and *summarising*.

Quoting, paraphrasing and summarising are all ways of taking notes about other people's words and ideas, and then using them in your essay. However, they have some important differences, which we explain below.

1 *Quoting*

Quoting is when you use the exact words that your source used. Generally, you only quote an author if the wording of the original source is important. You might be quoting a key part of a theory, or a particularly strong piece of evidence.

Quotes are always done in quotation marks to show that you are referring to the exact words of the original, and you also need to include the page number. For example:

> Yksisarvinen (2002) has argued that 'unicorns were critical to the economic prosperity of the state of New South Wales in the 1880s' (p. 49).

Too many quotes from the secondary literature, or quotes that are too long, can be a sign of a writer who isn't confident to put ideas into their own words. If you rely too heavily on quotations, the marker can't hear your 'writer's voice' and, by extension, your opinion. This is why quotes should only be used sparingly. In a research essay, for each paragraph of your own text you would typically quote only a few words, or perhaps a sentence, of someone else's writing. In some disciplines, it rare to include quotations at all. Ask your lecturer for advice.

2   Paraphrasing

Paraphrasing is when you refer to an idea that someone else has offered, but you talk about it in your own words. Use paraphrasing instead of direct quoting wherever possible.

Paraphrasing enables you to show you understand the material you are reading and makes it easier to slot other people's ideas into your sentences and paragraphs smoothly. Here's what a paraphrase might look like:

> Aon-Adharcach (2018) has argued that pixies were more significant to the economy than unicorns.

Paraphrasing can be an effort, but it is worth it as your voice and position can be more prominent in the writing.

Don't just use a thesaurus to swap out words. Not only does this tend to produce 'clunky' writing, it can introduce unexpected errors. Rewriting the example by picking words out of the synonyms offered by MS Word, for example, gives you a nonsense sentence:

> Aon-Adharcach (2018) has reasoned that sprites were more momentous to the budget than unicorns.

A better strategy is to cover up the quote and then try to explain it. If you find yourself getting stuck, that's often a sign that you don't understand the idea yet. Rather than focusing on individual words, keep researching and developing your understanding of the concepts and content. When you return to the paraphrase, it will come much more easily.

3   Summarising

Summarising is a lot like paraphrasing, but instead of giving a single idea in your own words, you give the gist of an entire section, chapter or journal article. Summaries are formatted and referenced in the same way as a paraphrase:

> The field of unicorn studies has generally moved on from the rivalries of the 1980s, though the relatively narrow focus of the field on a small subset of methodologies can still be considered a weakness (Kyaan, 2019).

4   Connecting and synthesising

While you are reading, keep an eye out for ways that your current source relates with other things you have read. If they reference that other source directly, it's particularly easy to see how they connect. Jot down any cross-references as they occur to you.

WORKSHEET 16 // PARAPHRASING AND CRITIQUING

If you struggle with quotations, paraphrases, summaries and critiques,
the following exercise can be helpful.

Create a table with a column each for the Source, Quote, Paraphrase, Critique and Summary.

1   Fill in the Source column.
2   Pick out as many quotes as you think you will use in your essay and write them in the 'Quote' column.
3   Now read the first quote, then cover it up and write a paraphrased version in the Paraphrase column.
4   Write down any questions, concerns, limitations or connections that occur to you about the quote, and put them in the Critique column.
5   Go through and complete a Paraphrase and Critique for each quote.
6   Look over the Paraphrases, and create a Summary.

Source	Quote	Paraphrase	Critique	Summary
Smith, J 2009, 'A brief history of cladistics', *Methods in Systematics*, vol. 6, no. 2, pp. 50–72.	'the focus of most of the work in this field has, erroneously, been on the application of parsimony-based methods' (p. 62)	Parsimony-based methods have received the bulk of the attention of researchers in this field.	He correctly identifies that this is where their attention is, but does not really examine why that is where they focus.	The field of cladistics has generally moved past the rivalries and controversies of the 1980s, though the relatively narrow focus of the field on a small subset of methodologies can still be considered a weakness.
	'long-branch attraction has been shown to be an issue for parsimony methods where some taxa are not closely related' (p. 70)	Parsimony tree building is affected by long-branch attraction in some instances.	This is a good point, but he doesn't say anything about how common this situation is in real-life analyses.	
	'though it is no longer characterised by animosity between its proponents, the field has nevertheless not resolved some of its core philosophical issues' (p. 72)	Philosophical issues remain unsolved in the field of cladistics.	Are the issues solvable? If they represent an irreconcilable difference with other methodological views, this might be asking too much.	

SOURCE Shaun Lehmann

WORKSHEET 16 // PARAPHRASING AND CRITIQUING

Here's a blank version you can use as a template.

Source	Quote	Paraphrase	Critique	Summary

When it comes to synthesising (bringing multiple sources together), these connections will help you find all the parts before trying to combine them.

5 *Critiquing*

Active reading means evaluating and analysing the source, as well as understanding and selecting from it. A critique doesn't necessarily mean you think there is anything wrong with the source. It might be a set of questions that you cannot answer, which will show you that you need to find another, different source. Noticing what is good, compelling or effective in a source is also a critique. Critique can also be positive!

Capture your own reactions while you read, so you can find them again when you need to incorporate critical thoughts into your essay.

Digital note-taking strategies

Storing information from your studies digitally means you can keep a copy of the ebook or PDF, any notes about it, all your drafts and lots of other information – all on a portable laptop. You can access all of it, at any time, anywhere. You can search, store, make notes and draft your essay, all from the same place. This is great when you have a few assignments that require a small number of sources.

Database tools

The most useful strategy is to build a notes database. Keep your lecture notes, class notes, details about individual assignments, reading notes, pictures and sound clips all in one place. There are lots of free options: some of these are apps you can use on multiple devices, so your notes are always accessible. See if your

Soon, however, you will have hundreds of sources on your desktop, and the challenge will become sorting, finding and managing the materials. We recommend software tools that can help you keep track of what you've found, and help you to find it again when you come to read it, use it to write your essay or cite it.

university has software you can use as part of your studies – sometimes these options are more secure and private than a free app.

Some people like the tactile sensation of writing in a notebook. There are some platforms that support optical character recognition (OCR), which means you can scan or take a photograph of your written notes and make them searchable.

Reference managers

To store the downloaded articles and books you have sourced, you might start investing time in a 'reference manager', like Zotero or EndNote online. These programs are usually available via your university, and the library or writing centre will run regular training sessions on them.

If you are just looking at a few sources for now, you can instead build folders to store and sort the material. Here are a few ideas to help you stay organised.

- Save your files, using names that you will recognise later. Include as many key terms as you can. 183875080ou9879.pdf is not useful, but Singh_Jones_2012_Unicorn_Economy_NSW_1880s.pdf is super.
- In your OneDrive, Dropbox, Google Drive or Desktop, create folders for each

class you are taking. Within that folder, make more folders for each assignment.

- Sort your sources, drafts or other files into the relevant folders.
- Keep adding to the folders as you go. Then you will always be able to find the material you need.

Key terms and tags

It's a good idea to build up a library of key terms or 'tags' in your note-taking software or your digital library. Tags (#hashtags) or keywords make searching easier and will help you cross-reference material, which is particularly useful for sources you'll be using over and over again. Tags also help you tell the difference between the many different 'economics essay' or 'history notes' files that start to float around when you've done more than one essay.

Here are some suggestions:

- Make tags for individual projects. We recommend tagging based on the class code (e.g. #eco101) or topic with the semester (#DerivativesSem2).
- Make tags for common tasks or actions. Any piece of information that might help you do something could have a tag related to that kind of task, e.g. #writing, #statistics, #maths, #grammar.
- Descriptive tags are key words used to describe a cluster or category of information. A category can be related to things (e.g. #fruit), places (#Canberra), type of information (#CensusData, #poems), people (#Marx), or anything really. Most good databases will bring up your previous tags as you type so that you don't end up with lots of versions of the same #fruit #fruits #Fruit (or misspelled #friut) tag.

- Make tags for how you feel about the information. Just like you tag social media posts with phrases about how you feel, you can use tags to show how you feel about information for your studies. Tags like #interesting, #boring, #wow, #hate and #annoying are surprisingly useful when you are trying to decide which bits of information you are going to bother to engage with in the time you have left before your essay is due!

Sorting and tagging your materials can take some time to set up; it is work best done when no urgent essays are due. It can also take time to learn new software, or to explore different options to find the one that works for you.

A database takes time and commitment to build, but has major benefits when you are rushing to finish an essay. If you have ever had to waste time looking for sources you found and seem to have lost again, you'll know what we mean.

8.5 TAKING NOTES THAT TURN INTO WRITING

Taking notes in the margins of an article or on a blank page is fine, but many people find using a notes template is more effective for connecting their notes to their essay writing. Instead of just jotting things down as they occur to you, you might want to spend some time setting things up so you take better quality notes that are more likely to be useful to you when you come back to use them for a research essay.

You can buy specific notebooks that already have a note-taking template, and most note-taking software will have similar features. Otherwise, you can make your own.

A good notes template will have the following features.

- It includes bibliographic information, and any other access information like dates, web addresses and page numbers. You will be already set up for your references, and can go back and check more information if you need to.
- It makes it easy to find the different quotes, notes and critiques you want to include.
- It records the notes in a way that will make sense to you later. Cryptic or illegible notes are not much use.
- It includes space for identifying themes, key words and recurrent patterns. Use this to make sure your notes are relevant to your essay question. The themes also work like an index to your notes, so you can find the information again. Tags are another good way to do this if you take notes digitally (see page 107).
- It makes it easy to compare notes from different articles to connect and synthesise information.
- There is space to record your own critiques, reactions and judgments. Do you think the source is trustworthy? How does it compare to other sources? What does it miss out? Is the source not relevant for this essay, but might be useful for another assessment later on?
- There is space for your summary. Always summarise when you are taking notes. If you leave the summary for when you are writing your draft, you will need to take a break to read the whole article again!
- It helps you turn notes into full academic sentences. Your notes will probably be written in shortened form, using abbreviations, symbols, arrows and diagrams. However, in your essay, you will

need to write in full academic sentences. You should always summarise your notes using full academic sentences. You can also use the 'note nuggets' strategy (see below).

If this sounds harder than just writing down everything that looks like it might be interesting – that's because it is! But it is also faster than copying everything out laboriously. Plus, your later writing self will thank you when you have clear, usable, searchable and scholarly notes just waiting to be brought together into an essay.

The Cornell method of note-taking

The Cornell method was invented about 60 years ago by Walter Pauk and appeared in his classic book *How to Study in College*. One of the reasons we like the Cornell method is that it helps you understand what notes are supposed to do, and all the thinking work you need to make them effective. It was designed for taking notes in lectures by hand, and provides space for your notes; margins for reactions, connections and comments; and a space for a summary.

Katherine has updated the template to work for taking notes from books and articles towards writing an essay or thesis. Even if your method of note-taking looks different, you need to be doing all of these academic tasks, so working through the template will help you build better notes.

The Cornell template includes:

- space for bibliographic information
- a column to record page numbers
- a column for themes and key words
- limited space to write notes, paraphrases, quotes and reflections, to help you be selective
- plenty of space to write a summary in full sentences at the bottom of the page.

Figure 6: Katherine's Cornell note-taking example

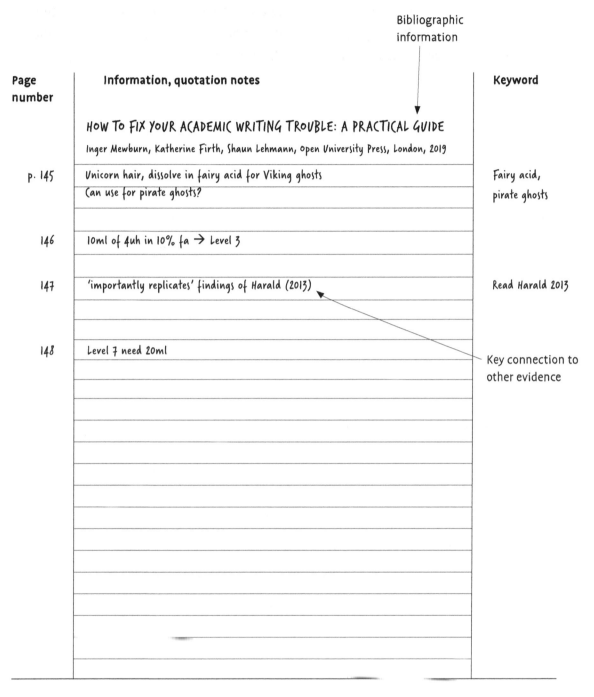

Bibliographic
information

Page number	Information, quotation notes	Keyword
	HOW TO FIX YOUR ACADEMIC WRITING TROUBLE: A PRACTICAL GUIDE Inger Mewburn, Katherine Firth, Shaun Lehmann, Open University Press, London, 2019	
p. 145	Unicorn hair, dissolve in fairy acid for Viking ghosts Can use for pirate ghosts?	Fairy acid, pirate ghosts
146	10ml of 4uh in 10% fa → Level 3	
147	'importantly replicates' findings of Harald (2013)	Read Harald 2013
148	Level 7 need 20ml	

Key connection to
other evidence

Summary:

In order to lay pirate ghosts, over 20ml of unicorn hair dissolved in fairy acid is
required (Harald 2013, Mewburn et al. 2019).

Full prose summary.
Can go straight into my
essay.

Source: Katherine Firth

WORKSHEET 17 // THE CORNELL METHOD OF NOTE-TAKING

You can photocopy this template to write by hand (we've provided a page for you to practise by hand and/or photocopy). You can make any lined notebook into a Cornell notebook with a ruler and pen, or build your own Cornell template in MS Excel or OneNote.

Project: _____

Notes page: _____

Page

Themes & Keywords

Summary

Source: Katherine Firth

Don't copy and paste your notes into your essay

Many students try to fill up their essay by copying and pasting phrases, sentences and paragraphs from sources, then trying to rewrite and shape these into their essay. This is a really bad idea for three reasons:

1   It's very hard to structure a strong and well-written essay from a patchwork of rewritten words. If you write freely first, you will be able to create a strong argument in your own voice.

2   It's very easy to copy and paste, which means your brain isn't working hard enough to select the important words that are worth quoting, or to judge there aren't any. This lack of hard work means you easily make mistakes, select weak evidence and possibly won't remember much of the information later.

3   Even if you try hard to rewrite the paragraphs and reference everything, you are not really writing it yourself. At best, this leads to wooden writing that doesn't 'flow', and it will not be original or well argued. Even if Turnitin doesn't flag it as being too close to the original texts, your lecturer will recognise that you have just 'remixed' your sources, instead of synthesising your own critical position

If you want to use text from other people as a starting point, refer to our section on sentence skeletons in Chapter 4, or use 'note nuggets' (below) to fill your page with useful text in your own words.

Create note nuggets

Instead of copying other people's paragraphs, you can write your own notes as 'note nuggets' – small 'nuggets' of text containing insights or ideas framed in 'academic speak', ready to be used in your essay.

> In each 'nugget', you capture your idea or the idea of another person, and you write it so well that it can be cut and pasted straight into your essay document. This is a powerful technique to avoid the blank page, and to start writing your essay while taking your notes.

Training yourself to write your notes as pre-formatted nuggets of your future essay is not difficult, and the rewards will be better thinking and quicker writing. This approach also helps you to avoid plagiarism because you are always writing about other peoples' ideas in your own words.

Write your note nuggets as whole sentences, each with a verb in it. For example, turn a note like '58% treatments for baldness' into a nugget by rewriting it with a verb like 'claims', 'argues' or 'shows':

shows 58% of treatments for baldness

That suddenly reminds you to explain who is doing the showing, and what they are showing:

Odoi (2009) **shows** 58% of treatments for baldness are unicorn hair.

Perhaps you are in a discipline (like science) where we don't tend to start sentences with an author's name. So instead you would write:

Previous studies of unicorn hair **have shown** that they comprise up to 58% of treatments for baldness on the market (Odoi, 2009).

As soon as you try to add a verb, you are forced to add subjects and objects. Before you know it, you've formed a whole sentence.

Later on, when you face the blank page of your essay, you can 'lift' sentences like these straight out of your notes and start to build more text around them.

Build a literature matrix

Most research essays require you to compare and contrast 10–20 sources, or even more. It can be hard to keep everything you read in your head, or to have to keep searching back through your pages and pages of notes.

One of the best ways to bring your notes into 'conversation' with other sources is a literature matrix. You can build a matrix in any software that allows you to build a table. But we strongly recommend you use MS Excel.

Here's how to start:

1   Set up your table with the name of each article you are using at the top of each column.
2   Use the rows to segment off topics (perhaps using the key themes you identified from your essay question or tags, or through using the Cornell note-taking method, described on page 108).
3   Then fill in what each author had to say about each topic. You can use 'note nuggets', written as full sentences with verbs, to fill in the cells and use them in your essay.
    See example in Table 3 below.

Then, when it comes time to write this section of your essay, you can read across all the rows to see how the insights from various authors might relate to each other.

Table 3: Literature matrix example

	'Unicorn products in the treatment of male pattern baldness' (Odoi, 2009)	'Unicorn blood: Uses in traditional folk remedies' (Ilgagsu, 2016)	'"There not be Unicorns": Dwindling populations and the production of hair products' (Jednorožec, 2018)
What is unicorn hair used for?	Odoi argues that unicorn hair accounts for 58% of all male pattern baldness remedies on the market.	Ilgagsu discusses the growing body of evidence on the effectiveness of ancient unicorn-blood remedies.	Jednorožec warns that the increasing demand for unicorn hair to treat male pattern baldness is putting pressure on wild populations.
What other uses are there for unicorn products?	Odoi claims that hair is a more important product then blood and makes more sustainable herd management.	Ilgagsu mostly focuses on blood in this paper but gives us some interesting information on other articles.	Jednorožec advocates for less use of unicorn products for all purposes.

WORKSHEET 18 // PRACTISE USING A LITERATURE MATRIX

Here are some tables where you can practise making a literature matrix.

	Source:	Source:	Source:	Source:
Theme 1				
Theme 2				
Theme 3				
Theme 4				
Theme 5				
Theme 6				

IN SUMMARY ...

* Not all evidence is the same!
  Make sure you are doing due
  diligence on the authors of each
  source and make considered
  judgments about how the format
  and age of the evidence might
  affect its validity in your essay.

* Taking notes is part of the writing
  process, so pay attention to how
  you are collecting and storing
  your notes. Use appropriate
  software to make the job easier,
  or use a good note-taking
  template.

* Wrangling your notes into an
  argument is the heart of the
  essay-writing process. Use a
  template or table to help you see
  relationships and patterns in the
  evidence you collect.

9

PLAN YOUR WAY TO (ALMOST) PERFECTION

When you were at school, your days were almost fully scheduled. Multiple times a day, a bell rang and your timetable and teachers told you to study, or to have a break. You did a lot of work in class, with extra, clearly defined tasks to do at home. You probably got feedback along the way, helping you to redraft your work, or understand what a concept meant. If you were at a regular job before studying, you had structure, plenty of meetings or shifts, and probably a boss to tell you what to do.

At university, a lot of the reading, research, writing and thinking – especially for essays – happens outside of class time. A full-time study load at uni is meant to be like having a full-time job. If a full-time load is four subjects per semester, then the university assumes you are spending an average of eight or more hours a week on each subject. If you have three contact hours in a subject (lectures, tutorials, workshops, practicals) then you are expected to spend at least five to six hours beyond that reading, researching and writing. Working outside the classroom on things like researching and writing essays can be a big part of that independent learning time.

Your life is also often more complicated at university. You might be balancing home responsibilities, a part-time job and extracurricular activities, then jumbling your studies into the mix.

The most effective students know that a good essay grade starts with having a good plan. The plan means you have enough time to do the tasks you need to do. It means you've done enough of the background work to be able to sit down and write. And it means you will be focused and able to concentrate when you are doing the work.

9.1 DO YOU KNOW HOW YOU ACTUALLY SPEND YOUR TIME?

It's worth tracking your time for a full week to see how it actually went. When did you wake up? When did you stop hitting the snooze button and actually get up? How much time did you spend revising for that test and did it take a lot longer than you expected? How much time do you spend commuting?

> Record your work week, whether that's 9 am – 5 pm Monday to Friday, or spread out in another way. How many hours do you actually spend on your uni work? The answer might shock you.

The worksheet below gives you an hourly template for a whole week. We know you might study on evenings or weekends, and that no two days might look the same.

For a week, track what you did in every

HOURLY SCHEDULE

Date:							
	Monday	Tuesday	Wednesday	Thursday	Friday	Saturday	Sunday
12:00 AM							
1:00 AM							
2:00 AM							
3:00 AM							
4:00 AM							
5:00 AM							
6:00 AM							
7:00 AM							
8:00 AM							
9:00 AM							
10:00 AM							
11:00 AM							
12:00 PM							
1:00 PM							
2:00 PM							
3:00 PM							
4:00 PM							
5:00 PM							
6:00 PM							
7:00 PM							
8:00 PM							
9:00 PM							
10:00 PM							
11:00 PM							

hour. Include sleeping, eating, commuting, getting ready, leisure, chores and paid work, as well as study tasks. Don't worry about a few minutes here or there.

When you have completed the weekly record, go back and add up how long you spent studying independently – including reading, taking notes, doing analysis and so on. Hopefully you found you were putting aside enough hours. A full-time study load usually requires about 40–45 hours per week.

Did it surprise you how long it took to do certain tasks?

9.2   THE POWER OF SELF-REFLECTION

If you did the time tracking exercise above, you'll have a good idea of how you're spending your week. What did it reveal about your patterns of study?

Students are often advised to start assessments early, to plan out their time carefully, and to not try to do their work at the last minute. You might have also been told to plan your essay paragraph by paragraph before you start writing. You might have been told that getting up early is more effective than staying up late. But if the 'commonsense' advice you've been given never worked for you, that is because it's advice that only works for *some* people.

People have different preferences around working under pressure, planning ahead, what time of day to work – and much more. It's important to work in a way that balances your own preferences and patterns for work, and allows you to get your work done on time in the least stressful way possible. We encourage you to be realistic: work smarter not harder.

Some people will also have to work with their physical and mental health, to ensure that their way of studying is compatible with

the way their brains and bodies work. Self-knowledge means making realistic plans that work for you, whether or not these look like other people's ways of working. Your university should have support structures in place to help you, whether through your lecturers, or an equity and inclusion centre. Support can include accessibility software, having more time to write essays and other accommodations. You will usually need to be your own advocate with health care providers and your university, so self-knowledge is also critical in setting up an access plan that will work for you.

University life gives you a lot of choices about how you work and when. Other than scheduled class times or group work, you can order your working patterns to suit yourself, and also work in some unexpected ways. You are free to include breaks, and even naps, into your work pattern.

You can also decide how you write, and what order you do certain steps in. For example, you can 'write from the middle', or 'write to find the plan'. You might find it's more effective for you to plan to write badly. You might even find it helps you to write a draft where you put everything that doesn't belong into your essay … and then go on to rewrite and edit. In the next section we talk about some unexpected ways to write.

9.3   WRITE TO FIND THE PLAN

Teachers often advocate planning everything in advance. The assumption behind this advice is that a plan will help you write a well-constructed essay that includes all the key points. But we question whether this advice always works.

> For lots of people, the most challenging part of the essay is starting. Sometimes, students will make elaborate plans, or read just one more article, to avoid having to deal with that big blank space on their laptop screen. If that sounds like you, you will probably find it unhelpful writing a bullet-point plan as a starting point. Likewise, just listing your headings doesn't fill up much blank space. Starting with a list also encourages you to put in too many 'points' and not enough 'argument'.

It can help to include actual writing in your planning process so, instead of making a plan, try writing a short piece that tells the story of your essay, or write a quick first draft that sketches out your ideas. This will encourage you to put your ideas into words, and put your words into sentences.

Write it fast

Often a good way to find out what you want to say is to try saying it – or writing it. Just get your ideas out onto a piece of paper where you can see them!

When you are trying to get ideas out, it's helpful to write them down as fast as you can, not as well as you can. Try setting a timer for five to ten minutes and answer this question: 'What am I trying to argue?' Your response should include the key ideas in your essay, and explain how they fit together.

Because you are writing to find the plan, you don't need to worry too much about whether the writing is elegant, or whether you have all the details. You want a big-picture sketch. It's okay if the writing is ungrammatical, or 'bad writing'. This is about the *ideas*.

People are often amazed at how much they can write in such a short amount of time, and with so little pre-planning. In fact, they don't believe it's possible without trying it. So we've given you some space to have a go and see that it really does work!

Make a really, really rough draft

If you are used to having one go to write a good essay (like in an exam), it can be liberating to remember that your first draft doesn't have to be very good. No one else needs to read it! Give yourself permission to write really badly. Anne Lamott, in her book *Bird by Bird*, talks about the 'shitty first draft'. It can be rambling, too long, too short, full of mistakes. That's okay. That doesn't mean it's not useful writing. 'Badly written text' gets the ideas on paper where you can start to work them around. First you have to discover your ideas, then you have to put them into words. Sometimes you have to see an idea on the page before you can evaluate if it's valid or valuable. Once you have good ideas on the page, that's the time to turn it into better writing.

> A fast and messy first draft is, surprisingly, often much easier to tidy up later than trying to write it perfectly the first time. Many very efficient writers write too many words and then cut back – this may sound inefficient, but if the words come fast and are easy to edit, it actually takes less time and energy than trying to get it perfect the first time.

WORKSHEET 20 // WRITE FAST, WRITE YOUR ARGUMENT

'What am I trying to argue in this essay?'

This page is for you to write really fast for five minutes. Write as fast as you can,
not as well as you can. Do not stop for word choice: put whatever word you think of first,
or write 'I don't know what to call this', and keep going. Later you can go back and choose
what word works best.

_____

_____

_____

_____

_____

_____

_____

_____

_____

_____

_____

_____

_____

_____

_____

_____

_____

_____

_____

_____

_____

_____

_____

_____

Some people find that it's easier to write a first draft in a different program from their word-processing software. Use your phone to write a draft in your notes, use a voice-to-text app (or Google Docs) to record yourself speaking the essay, or write your essay as if you were writing an email to someone. Or draw a diagram – we've got some suggestions in Chapter 4.

After a break, maybe even a good night's sleep, you can come back and rewrite it. You can use our strategies in Chapters 5–7 to edit it and make it beautiful enough to submit.

If you just finished high school, then you are probably pretty good at sitting down with a pen and paper, and a timer, and writing an essay quickly. Universities expect you to do further work, and use more research, than in an exam essay. However, your old tactics can still be a good way to quickly produce a clear first draft in a short amount of time. If this is your preferred way, try writing your first draft by hand. As you type your handwritten essay up onto your computer, you will see where you can improve the writing, or add more details or evidence – plus you can do the work of formatting and checking your spelling!

You might think of yourself as a 'good writer' and shy away from writing in a way that feels messy or imperfect. But if you sit down to write and are 'stuck', or you write well but painfully slowly, you might find this rough-draft strategy helpful.

Write what it isn't

Sometimes it's hard to find clarity among all the ideas you generate when you write quickly. Sometimes it's easier to focus on what the essay will NOT include. To do this:

1   Check back to your essay question. Does it specify anything that you can exclude?
2   Identify any ideas that are weak, not strictly relevant or that you don't have good evidence for.
3   Try writing a list of theories, writers, facts or whatever else might not belong in this essay.

Sometimes your 'not list' can be used to form useful signposting language in the essay, for instance:

> In this essay I argue for the usefulness of unicorn hair in treating plantar fasciitis, but the specific uses of unicorn hair for other muscle injuries **is beyond the scope of this paper**.

Keep the list close by as you write to help you stay on track.

9.4   FOCUS AND CREATE A 'FLOW STATE'

Mihaly Csikszentmihalyi is famous for describing the 'flow state': where you are so focused on your work that you lose track of time. Flow can be achieved in many different activities, but when you are working on an essay, it's that feeling you get when writing becomes almost effortless.

It can seem like 'flow' just happens for you sometimes, yet at other times it's really hard to achieve. But the science says there are some ways to make flow more likely.

WORKSHEET 21 // WHAT MY ESSAY IS NOT ABOUT

This page is for what your essay is **not** about. Start with the sentence 'I am not trying to ...' and then free-write the rest, or just make a list of all the 'nots'.

_____

_____

_____

_____

_____

_____

_____

_____

_____

_____

_____

_____

_____

_____

_____

_____

_____

_____

_____

_____

_____

_____

_____

_____

_____

_____

_____

_____

How to focus

Here are some top tips to make flow happen more reliably.

1 Shut out (unhelpful) distractions

Even if you are working in a noisy or busy setting, you can take some actions to avoid distractions. Turn notifications and alarms off on your phone and computer. It's hard to focus if you are getting pinged every time someone posts a gif to the group chat!

If you are working in a place where you will be regularly interrupted by friends or family, find other places to study. Your local library or the uni library after hours are often excellent places. A café works if you can afford to buy a coffee or two. Maybe you can negotiate a time or a signal that helps other people know that they need to wait to talk to you – put your headphones on, shut your door or make a sign!

> Lots of people find that the sounds around them are distracting, but the sounds they create are okay. Because your brain can tune out an input stream it decides isn't very important, background music or white noise might not be too distracting. While some people find music with words is helpful, others dislike music with lyrics. Some like the soothing sounds of café chatter or falling rain; others like classical music or film scores. Find out what works for you. Every kind of soundscape is available online, via streaming or in apps.

2 Don't try to multitask

Humans don't actually multitask; we just switch our attention rapidly. Most of what people call 'multitasking' is actually rapid switching. All switching is fatiguing and distracting, and will erode your flow state.

In writing, this kind of switching is particularly costly as it takes time to reorient yourself to the task at hand. Reading, planning, writing and editing are common tasks that people try to switch between. Instead of doing them all at once, pick one task and do it for a 'chunk' of time. Work out whether your task is to be reading, making a plan, writing a first draft, editing your draft or formatting your bibliography. See the section on page 124 on the Pomodoro Technique for how to do this.

If you have a great idea for another task, don't stop what you are doing and switch tasks. It's more effective to write the idea down in a notebook and then get back to the current task. You can review your great ideas in a break, and decide when you will focus on each of them, rather than leapfrogging from task to task.

3 Don't let your body distract you

If you are tired, thirsty, in pain or busting for the loo, you won't be able to focus very well. Check that your desk and chair are comfortable, that you can easily see the screen, and that you have had enough water and eaten regular meals. Schedule in breaks. Look away from the screen. Have a bit of a stretch. Drink some more water. This will stop you from making yourself sick or injured by studying. Headaches, wrist and back pain, and eye strain are all common study injuries!

If you are falling asleep at your computer, you probably need a short nap. In your day-to-day life, try to get enough sleep, eat regular meals and do regular exercise. Go to see the doctor if you aren't feeling well so you can get better, and perhaps apply for an extension. You can't focus if you are too sick!

People with long-term illnesses or disabilities know that their body or brain can make it hard to focus, or to focus for extended amounts of time. Talk to your university disability and equity team about getting reasonable adjustments – you might just need a bit more time or some other support to make it through.

4 Make a reasonable plan

No-one can work for 18 hours a day, six days a week and be fully focused. Most people find writing for two to four hours a day, five days a week is a reasonable pace, though you could rearrange those hours so you did a longer block for a few days, and then took a longer break.

Set a timer when you work to get a realistic idea of how long things take for you, like reading an article or writing a paragraph. This knowledge will help you avoid rushing at the end.

Balance out writing essays with work that needs less brain power – like formatting your bibliography, checking your emails, rewatching a lecture to revise, or going to the library to return your books.

We're not fans of all-nighters. They tend to be stressful and inefficient. Worse, they are often used as a psychological bullying tactic to make other students feel bad. As we show in

the next section, research shows it's much more efficient to get a good night's sleep anyway.

Even if you like the feeling of a deadline push, check out the advice below on 'last-minute' writers, to stay productive – not rushed.

5 Schedule in spaces to think away from the desk

Your brain is obviously working when you are reading, planning, taking notes, writing and editing. However, most academic work also involves other skills, like coming up with ideas, problem solving, judgment and processing. It's time for these other skills to come online when you get 'stuck' and stop making progress.

You probably have already experienced having a great idea in the shower or while doing the washing up. You may have also experienced the way that something that seemed difficult to fix when you were at the computer is much easier when you come back after a walk with the dog, a trip to the gym or cooking dinner.

There are actually reasons why doing something else helps you get unstuck. Unfinished business hangs around in your brain 'on the backburner'. You might get a nagging feeling that you forgot to pick up milk from the shops, and you get a similar low-level itch about an essay you have started, if you start ahead of the deadline – deciding on your question, doing some basic reading and going to the lectures. By the time you come to work seriously on your essay, you will have already been turning the ideas over in your mind for some time. This tends to mean you've made a lot of progress even before you sit down and focus!

Another reason is that creativity and problem solving are most effective when your brain can be a bit 'fuzzy'. When you put your brain into 'low-attention mode', it doesn't stop thinking – it just comes at the issue from a different angle, or puts two things together that might not obviously connect. That's when you get that light bulb 'aha!' moment. By thinking about other things, or about nothing at all, your brain gets a chance to work in a fuzzy way.

Use a time-box method like the Pomodoro Technique

One way to stay focused, avoid switching problems, schedule regular breaks and keep track of how long tasks take you is to use a 'time-boxing' strategy. Time boxing is where you try to focus on one task for a nominated stretch of time, and then take a quick break.

The most famous time-box technique is the Pomodoro Technique. It is very simple to implement. You set a timer for 25 minutes, and focus on one task until the alarm goes off. You reset the timer for five minutes. You take a break or do something else. When the alarm sounds again, you start your next block of work. You repeat this pattern for up to two hours, when you take a much longer break.

Here is an example plan for a focused morning of work that uses the Pomodoro Technique as a basis for building blocks of productive time. We think most people will be able to finish a short essay if they do this every morning for a week.

Table 4: Example Pomodoro Technique plan

25 minutes	Write your essay plan.
5 minutes	Stretch. Refill your water bottle. Text your mum.
25 minutes	Write your introduction paragraph.
5 minutes	Go buy a coffee. Check social media while in the queue.
25 minutes	Write your context paragraph.
5 minutes	All that hydration has an effect! Go to the loo.
25 minutes	Review your introduction and context paragraph. Edit the text. Make notes for what you need to change next time.
Longer break	Lunch break!

NOTE The 'Pomodoro Technique' was invented by Francesco Cirillo in the late 1980s. 'Pomodoro' means 'tomato' in Italian; Cirillo named his technique after the tomato-shaped timer he used when he was a university student.

WORKSHEET 22 // PLAN YOUR TIME WITH THE POMODORO TECHNIQUE

Now make your own Pomodoro schedule.

25 minutes	
5 minutes	
25 minutes	
5 minutes	
25 minutes	
5 minutes	
25 minutes	
Longer break	

9.5 WORK WHILE YOU SLEEP!

Your full-time study is meant to be a full-time job, and you probably have a part-time job on top of this. This means you need to use your downtime and off-time to make progress on your writing. We are not suggesting that you work all the time – far from it! Having a nap or a good night's sleep can be part of your overall level-up strategy.

> There are lots of different ways of looking after yourself, like having a meal, doing exercise, doing chores, having a shower, hanging out with friends or playing a game. Sleep is basically a health potion that makes all of these strategies work better.

Scientists recommend sleep and rest as a powerful productivity hack. There are three ways this works.

1 Sleep and rest make you more alert

Trying to work when you are exhausted, hungry, thirsty or sick is a bad idea. Take a nap, have a snack or go see a doctor. When you are refreshed, come back and your work will go much faster and be a lot better. Going without sleep makes you tired, and when you are tired, you make bad decisions. If you pull an all-nighter before an exam, some studies have shown that you are too impaired to drive a car, and that it can lower your marks by as much as a whole grade.

2 Sleep and rest give you a chance for your brain to solve problems

Sleep is a great way to spend some time away from the computer and do other kinds of thinking, like creative problem solving. What's more, when you are asleep, your brain is doing a lot of reorganising. It arranges and connects information it thinks is important, and discards information it has decided is excess. So when you wake up in the morning after a good night's sleep with REM and deep-sleep phases, it's like your brain tidied the desk overnight and you can easily put your hands on the important information. (Rapid eye movement (REM) sleep is where you have dreams, and deep sleep is when it is hardest for you to wake up.)

3 Sleep gives you 'critical distance' from your work

When you are focused on the detail, it can be hard to step back and see the big picture. To level up your essay, you must regularly step back and assess your essay from your lecturer's point of view. Stepping away from the desk by having a good night's sleep, going to a yoga class or spending an hour playing a video game literally takes you, your body and your mind somewhere else. When you come back to your laptop, you can often see your work in a new light.

Taking a break and then picking your work up again is also useful for longer term memory recall. Your brain makes a judgment between 'things we need to know about now but can then forget' and 'things we need to know about in the medium or long term'. If you start working on your essay the day before it is due, watching the lectures for the first time, doing the readings, writing the essay and handing it in, then your brain will often forget about it pretty quickly. If you revisit the essay over days or a couple of weeks, then you are more likely to get the knowledge, ideas and concepts into your medium-term memory. If you then revisit the ideas again for the end of semester exams, or in a later subject, they will probably end up in your long-term memory, and you'll have that information for life.

9.6   EFFECTIVE 'LAST-MINUTE WRITERS'

> If you always find yourself writing down to the wire, you are probably a 'last-minute writer'. This means you find the pressure of deadlines really motivates you. As long as your work is submitted on time, there is nothing wrong with completing the work nearer the deadline. But there are some techniques to make sure your work is not rushed, and doesn't have to be submitted late or unfinished.

Successful 'last-minute writers' are not starting hours before the assignment is due. Although they sit down at their desk as the deadline is looming, they have prepared earlier. Successful 'last-minute writers' have already generated fully formed thoughts, based on evidence they have already gathered, and organised in high-quality notes that can be accessed efficiently during the writing (see Chapter 8).

Generate fully formed thoughts by researching earlier

If you're someone who tends to write your essays late, you need to make sure that you aren't also trying to research late. It's very difficult to write fast when you are constantly stopping and starting to look for sources or check your facts. It is even harder when you happen to come across sources that invalidate or challenge things you have said, so you have to rewrite a lot of existing material.

By moving your research phase earlier, you can build an understanding of your essay topic. This way, when you sit down to write, you will already have quite a bit of knowledge about what others think on the topic, what your own views are, and how these approaches interact. Think of it like questing in a game – taking time to collect items and weapons before you get into the boss fight. Here are a few tips for the last-minute writer:

- If there are multiple questions you could choose, make your choice as quickly as possible. There are no 'right' answers, so just go for it – all the questions are good questions.
- Get your books and articles early, and start reading them.
- Think about what you already know about the topic from your lectures and tutorials.

This approach works best when you keep good notes and store the items you read somewhere where you can find them again.

A sensible version of 'the last minute'

A sensible version of 'last-minute' writing does not actually mean the final 60 seconds!

> First of all, be realistic about how long it typically takes you to write and edit an essay. If it takes you eight hours, then trying to get it done in four will only end in tears. If it typically takes you four hours, don't try to cram it into two! There is no 'correct' amount of time to write an essay; we are all different. This is why we advocated self-knowledge earlier! Don't descend into a shame spiral when you fail to deliver on time or achieve the result you were after. Failure is a chance to gain self-knowledge about what you are capable of doing – and what you are not. It's important to know what works for you so you can reliably produce writing to a deadline.

Usually we recommend aiming to be done with your work a full 24–48 hours before it is due, but any amount of time that means you can have a good break from the essay and still read over it one last time will be plenty. Editing immediately after you finish writing tends to result in you seeing what you thought you said, rather than what you actually said, so it's best to have a break before editing. (We give some practical editing tips in Chapter 7).

Give yourself some time to upload your essay too. There are often technical challenges, and remember that getting your work in late can lose you significant marks at some universities.

IN SUMMARY ...

* Knowing yourself is the secret to effective planning. Know if you are an early bird or a last-minute writer. Find out how long it takes you to do various tasks and make a plan that is reasonable for you.

* Give yourself permission to write badly to get ideas out onto the page and start planning, and then move on to making the writing 'good'. Get a sense of what doesn't need to be in your essay, and then you'll have an idea of what to cut or what to avoid.

* Write a quick first draft, rather than cutting and pasting lots of quotes, or writing a list-style plan that has too many points and not enough focus.

* Don't lose sight of the need to have a balanced life: your brain sometimes works better when you are not forcing it to think hard all the time. Rest is critical to your ability to level up.

* Work in timed bursts to conserve energy and maintain focus. Universities usually have excellent wellbeing programs that support you with developing self-awareness, mindfulness and self-care. Tap into those resources.

AFTERWORD:
DEVELOPING YOUR WRITING BEYOND ESSAYS

We hope our advice has helped you write killer essays – what is next? Most books will emphasise that you practise, practise, practise. This advice is correct to a point. The more skilled you get, the more you will enjoy writing and the more motivated you will be to write, leading you to practise even more, and creating a virtuous circle. It's true that practice does matter, but it has to be the right kind of practice.

> Be ambitious: writing across genres and in different formats will help you develop skills that will translate back into your essays, but also into your professional life beyond university.

Here are some ideas.

1   Write when you don't have to write

If you are always writing to deadline, under pressure, you will always be writing when you are stressed. This can be unpleasant, and create an unhealthy relationship between the act of writing and your state of mind. This is why many people have trouble starting an essay: they dread going back into a headspace they know is no fun. So create opportunities for low-stakes writing. Writing in a daily diary, or journalling, is a good way to start. Or start writing long letters to your parents

or grandparents; they will love it and might send you extra cake, money or letters in return!

2   Write for the public

Offer articles to your university newspapers and magazines, or to blogs on your niche interests. Writing for a public audience is higher stakes, but it can also be exciting. Audiences for public writing are different from markers – they are reading in their spare time and so looking for entertainment. Some platforms have editors who will help you think about how to keep a reader engaged by rewriting your piece. Be humble and grateful to your editor. Put your ego aside and use this opportunity to learn. Good editors will help you correct habitual errors and bring out the best in your writing.

3   Edit Wikipedia pages

Correcting other people's writing (and errors) is satisfying and contributes to a better world. There are rules around what makes a good Wikipedia page, so make sure you familiarise yourself with them before starting, so your edits do not get rejected out of hand. There are a range of wikis out there, including computer game wikis, so find one that fits your niche interest. The world needs educated people like you donating your time to make us all smarter.

4   Enter a writing competition

Having a goal for your writing project is always desirable. It's even better if that goal is to win some money or a prize at the end of all that effort! Look for short-form essay competitions with word counts of the same length as the essays you have to write for uni. There are lots of writing competitions out there. However, most competitions have a lot of entrants, so don't take any lack of success as rejection. See it as practice that was a reward in itself.

5   Write with a buddy

You won't have a teacher and class time to give you external pressure to focus and write beyond your university courses. One good system is to find yourself a 'writing buddy'. Having a buddy system keeps you both accountable, and motivates you to do the work. For example, Inger wrote the first draft of this section and Katherine wrote the section about paragraphs while sitting together in the State Library of Victoria café. We worked using the Pomodoro Technique outlined in Section 9.4 of this book. During a two-hour session, we managed to write almost a whole chapter of content. So having a buddy really pays off.

> **EASTER EGG**
>
> * An Easter Egg is a hidden, secret extra that you can find in a video game if you know where to look. Most of the made-up examples in this book also have made-up author names, which are words for 'unicorn' in different languages – according to Google Translate. From Albanian to Yoruba and many languages in between ... see if there are any you recognise!

REFERENCE LIST

Archibald, Jo-Ann, Jenny Lee-Morgan, Jason De Santolo and Linda Tuhiwai Smith, eds. *Decolonizing Research: Indigenous storywork as methodology*. London: Zed Books, 2019.

Baird, Benjamin, Jonathan Smallwood, Michael D. Mrazek, Julia W.Y. Kam, Michael S. Franklin and Jonathan W. Schooler. 'Inspired by distraction: Mind wandering facilitates creative incubation'. *Psychological Science* 23, no. 10 (2012): 1117–1122. <http://doi.org/10.1177/0956797612446024>.

Bane, Rosanne. 'The writer's brain: What neurology tells us about teaching creative writing'. *Creative Writing: Teaching Theory and Practice* 2, no. 1 (February 2010), 41–50.

Barros, Luiz Otávio. *The Only Academic Phrasebook You'll Ever Need: 600 examples of academic language*. Scotts Valley, CA: Createspace Independent Publishing Platform, 2016.

Becker, Howard S. *Writing for Social Scientists: How to start and finish your thesis, book, or article*. Chicago: University of Chicago Press, 2008.

Boice, Robert. *Professors as Writers: A self-help guide to productive writing*. Stillwater, OK: New Forums, 1990.

Booth, Wayne C., Gregory G. Colomb, Joseph M. Williams, Joseph Bizup and William T. Fitzgerald. *The Craft of Research*. 4th ed. Chicago: University of Chicago Press, 2016.

Cirillo, Francesco. 'The Pomodoro Technique'. Accessed 7 July 2020. <https://francescocirillo.com/pages/pomodoro-technique>.

Cook, John, Naomi Oreskes, Peter T. Doran, William R.L. Anderegg, Bart Verheggen, Edward W. Maibach, J. Stuart Carlton *et al.* 'Consensus on consensus: A synthesis of consensus estimates on human-caused global warming'. *Environmental Research Letters* 11, no. 4 (2016): 048002. <http://doi.org/10.1088/1748-9326/11/4/048002>.

Cottrell, Stella. *The Study Skills Handbook*. 7th ed. London: Red Globe, 2019.

Covey, Stephen R. *The 7 Habits of Highly Effective People*. London: Simon & Schuster, 2013.

Csikszentmihalyi, Mihaly. *Finding Flow: The psychology of engagement with everyday life*. New York: Basic Books, 1997.

DiMaggio, Paul J. 'Comments on "What theory is not"'. *Administrative Science Quarterly* 40, no. 3 (1995): 391–397. <http://doi.org/10.2307/2393790>.

Durmer, Jeffrey S. and David F. Dinges. 'Neurocognitive consequences of sleep deprivation'. *Seminars in Neurology* 25, no. 1 (2005): 117–129. <http://doi.org/10.1055/s-2005-867080>.

Hershner, Shelley D. and Ronald D. Chervin. 'Causes and consequences of sleepiness among college students'.

Nature and Science of Sleep 6 (2014): 73–84. <http://doi.org/10.2147/NSS.S62907>.

Ishikawa, Kaoru. *Guide to Quality Control*. Tokyo: Asian Productivity Organization, 1972.

Joki, Kimberly. 'A scary-easy way to help you find passive voice!' *Grammarly Blog*, 12 October 2014. <https://www.grammarly.com/blog/a-scary-easy-way-to-help-you-find-passive-voice/>.

Jones, Lawrence, Christopher Sciamanna and Erik Lehman. 'Are those who use specific complementary and alternative medicine therapies less likely to be immunized?' *Preventive Medicine* 50, no. 3 (2010): 148–154. <http://doi.org/10.1016/j.ypmed.2009.12.001>.

King, Stephen. *On Writing: A memoir of the craft*. New York: Scribner, 2002.

KU Medical Center. 'Teaching and learning technologies: Blackboard rubrics'. Accessed 14 July 2020. <http://www.kumc.edu/information-resources/teaching-and-learning-technologies/our-services/blackboard/blackboard-rubrics.html>.

Lamott, Anne. *Bird by Bird: Instructions on writing and life*. Edinburgh: Canongate, 2020.

Luker, Kristin. *Salsa Dancing in the Social Sciences: Research in an age of info-glut*. Cambridge, MA: Harvard University Press, 2008.

Mewburn, Inger. '5 ways to declutter your writing'. *The Thesis Whisperer*, 4 November 2010. <https://thesiswhisperer.com/2010/11/04/5-ways-to-declutter-your-writing/>.

Mewburn, Inger, Katherine Firth and Shaun Lehmann. *How to Fix Your Academic Writing Trouble: A practical guide*. London: Open University Press, 2019.

Murray, Rowena. *How to Write a Thesis*. London: McGraw Hill Education, 2011.

Oxford English Dictionary. 'argument, n.'. Accessed 9 February 2020. <http://www.oed.com>.

Pauk, Walter, and Ross J.Q. Owens. *How to Study in College*. 11th ed. Boston: Cengage Learning, 2014.

Read, Siew Hean. *Academic Writing Skills for International Students*. London: Red Globe, 2018.

Strunk, William Jr. and E.B. White. *The Elements of Style*. 4th ed. Boston: Allyn and Bacon, 1999.

Sutton, Robert I. and Barry M. Staw. 'What theory is not'. *Administrative Science Quarterly* 40, no. 3 (1995): 371–384. <http://doi.org/10.2307/2393788>.

Swales, John M. and Christine B. Feak. *Academic Writing for Graduate Students: Essential tasks and skills*. Ann Arbor, MI: University of Michigan Press, 2004.

Sword, Helen. *Stylish Academic Writing*. Cambridge, MA: Harvard University Press, 2012.

Sword, Helen. *The Writer's Diet*. Auckland: Auckland University Press, 2015.

Thacher, Pamela V. 'University students and the "all nighter": Correlates and patterns of students' engagement in a single night of total sleep deprivation'. *Behavioral Sleep Medicine* 6, no. 1 (2008): 16–31. <http://doi.org/10.1080/15402000701796114>.

Thomson, Pat and Barbara Kamler. *Detox Your Writing: Strategies for doctoral researchers.* New York: Routledge, 2016.

Thomson, Pat and Barbara Kamler. *Writing for Peer Reviewed Journals: Strategies for getting published.* Abingdon, UK: Routledge, 2012.

Turabian, Kate L. *A Manual for Writers of Research Papers, Theses, and Dissertations: Chicago style for students and researchers.* 9th edition. Edited by Wayne C. Booth, Gregory G. Colomb, Joseph M. Williams, Joseph Bizup and William T. FitzGerald. Chicago: University of Chicago Press, 2018.

Williams, Joseph M. and Joseph Bizup. *Style: The basics of clarity and grace.* 5th ed. New York: Pearson, 2014.

Wiseman, Richard. *Night School: Wake up to the power of sleep.* London: Spin Solutions, 2014.

Wohl, Hannah and Gary A. Fine. 'The active skim: Efficient reading as a moral challenge in postgraduate education'. *Teaching Sociology* 45, no. 3 (2017): 220–227. <https://doi.org/10.1177/0092055X17697770>.

Wurman, Richard S., Loring Leifer, David Sume and Karen Whitehouse. *Information Anxiety 2.* 2nd ed. Indianapolis: Que, 2001.

Zinsser, William. *On Writing Well: The classic guide to writing nonfiction.* New York: Harper Perennial, 2016.

RECOMMENDED READING

GETTING STARTED

Becker, Howard S. *Writing for Social Scientists: How to start and finish your thesis, book, or article.* Chicago: University of Chicago Press, 2008.

Cottrell, Stella. *The Study Skills Handbook.* 5th ed. London: Red Globe, 2019.

Goodson, Patricia. *Becoming an Academic Writer: 50 exercises for paced, productive, and powerful writing.* 2nd ed. Thousand Oaks, CA: Sage, 2016.

Pauk, Walter, and Ross J.Q. Owens. *How to Study in College.* 11th ed. Boston: Cengage Learning, 2014.

Read, Siew Hean. *Academic Writing Skills for International Students.* London: Red Globe, 2018.

Williams, Joseph M. and Joseph Bizup. *Style: The basics of clarity and grace.* 5th ed. New York: Pearson, 2014.

GOING FURTHER (FOR CREATIVE AND NON-FICTION WRITERS)

King, Stephen. *On Writing: A memoir of the craft.* New York: Scribner, 2002.

Zinsser, William, *On Writing Well: The classic guide to writing nonfiction.* New York: Harper Perennial, 2016.

GOING FURTHER (FOR POST-GRADUATES AND HONOURS STUDENTS)

Mewburn, Inger, Katherine Firth and Shaun Lehmann. *How to Fix Your Academic Writing Trouble: A practical guide.* London: Open University Press, 2019.

Murray, Rowena. *How to Write a Thesis.* London: McGraw Hill Education, 2011.

Swales, John M. and Christine B. Feak. *Academic Writing for Graduate Students: Essential tasks and skills.* Ann Arbor, MI: University of Michigan Press, 2004.

Sword, Helen. *The Writer's Diet.* Auckland: Auckland University Press, 2015.

ACKNOWLEDGMENTS

We'd like to thank our publisher, Phillipa McGuinness, Harriet McInerney and the team at NewSouth, as well as our amazing editor, Emma Driver.

Thanks also to the people who read and gave feedback on early drafts of the book, particularly Dr Catherine Frieman from the Australian National University and Dr Matthew Jones from the University of Greenwich.

We'd like to make some personal thank yous too.

Inger: I'd like to thank my husband Luke for always being my personal cheer squad and writing-time coffee maker. I'd also like to thank my son Brendan for occasionally listening to my advice on writing and doing the hard work of becoming quite a good writer himself. (Thank you Brendan, so much, for helping on the last, painful copy edit of this book.) Thanks to the many people who wrote the books that taught me to be a writer, and to the students who shared their problems with me. Big shout-out to Professor Pat Thomson, blog sister, for teaching me so much about writing in addition to being a great friend and role model.

Katherine: I'd like to thank the many students who workshopped this advice with me over the last 15 years. I learned so much from you all. Thank you to my co-authors on the other books I was writing at the same time, who supported me as I juggled this project along with theirs. A particular shout-out to my partner and partner-in-writing Andreas who always understands when it's book crunch-time. And finally, thanks to Jessamy Gleeson, writing wrangler and general book boss, who keeps my projects in line.

Shaun: I'd like to give my thanks to all of the students who have come to my writing consultations or attended my workshops over the years; I have learned so much from all of you. I'd also like to thank my co-authors, who have been wonderful to work with, and a constant source of support and new perspectives. Finally, I'd like to thank my colleagues at the Australian National University and the University of New South Wales who have always been encouraging and generous with their time.

Finally, thank you to you, the reader. We hope you feel empowered and inspired by this book to go out and write some awesome essays.

INDEX

academic English *see also* language
  conventions 28, 61, 70, 72, 78, 85
  English, types of 76–78
  grammar *see* grammar
  improving 74–76, 78
  language barriers 71–74
  literary English and 77
  online English and 77–78
  spoken English and 76–77
active voice 67
apostrophes 75
argument 13–14, 37, 38, 58 *see also* essay structure
  academic 13, 38–39
  checklist 36
  critical judgment 40
  essay introduction, in 14
  evidence 13–14, 93 *see also* evidence
  module paragraphs 34
  planning using paragraphs 35
  position, taking 39–40
  'scholarly consensus' 39–40
  sentence skeletons 56–57
  'sides', identification of 39
  signposting language 65
  truth claims 40–43
  unusual 20
audience 6
  lecturers 7, 11–22

Barros, Luiz Otávio 56
  The Only Academic Phrasebook You'll Ever Need 56
'bedraggled daisy diagram' search strategy 96–97
body paragraphs 26–30, 37
  argument planning 35
  'chunk of thinking' approach 28
  conclusion sentences 29
  evidence 29
  explanation 29
  length 28
  link-forward sentences 29
  modules 34–36
  own words, using 29
  PIE (Point, Illustration, Explanation) 28
  signposting 66
  structure 28
  TEEL (Topic, Evidence, Explanation, Link) 28

  topic sentences 28
  worksheet 30, 35

capitalisation 85
colloquialisms 76–77
collusion 11, 75
conclusion 31, 34, 36, 37
  bigger picture breadth 31
  limitations of analysis, highlighting 31
  purpose 31
  signposting 66–67
  worksheet 32
Cornell method of note-taking 108–110
Cottrell, Stella 75
  The Study Skills Handbook 75
Covey, Stephen 91
  The 7 Habits of Highly Effective People 91
The Craft of Research 24
'criterion-referenced' assessment 7

dashes 86

editing 15, 70, 79–89
  argument 80
  capitalisation 85
  common editing mistakes 87–88
  commonly confused words 83, 85
  dashes 86
  due date and time 80
  feedback, using 89
  final stages 83–87
  formatting and style 86
  handing essay in 86–87
  italics 85
  numbers 85
  priorities for, setting 79–80
  quotations 85
  reading work aloud 79
  software 83, 87
  sources, checking 80
  time for 79, 87, 89
  word length, reducing 80–83
  worksheet 84
ESL students 64, 68, 71–74
  article errors 74
  direct translation problems 73
  grammar issues 72
  'interference' between

  mother tongue and English 72–73, 78
  local academic conventions 72
  tense use 73–74
  using English every day 74
essay drafts 61, 118
essay marking 7–8, 10
  'blind' marking 12
  'criterion-referenced' assessment 7
  feedback from lecturers 8–9, 10
  grade bracket criteria 8
  marker's viewpoint 11–12
  'norm-referenced' assessment 7
  purpose of grades 8
  quality and consistency of markers 8
  rubric 7 *see also* rubrics
  unfair grades 9
essay questions 12–13
  'compare and contrast' 43
  'discuss' 44
  implied argument 12, 13 *see also* argument
  rubrics *see* rubrics
  structure of essay within 43
  'to what degree' 44
  topic 12–13
  truth claims and 41–43
  'unpopular' 20
  yes/no 43–44
  your understanding of 12
essay structure *see also* argument; body paragraphs; conclusion; introduction
  diagrams 45, 48–55
  feather diagram 48, 49
  fishbone diagram 50, 51
  LATCH theory of information 45, 46, 58
  quadrant diagram 54, 55
  spider diagram 52, 53
  theory, use of 57
  within question, finding 43–45, 58
  worksheets 49, 51, 53
evidence
  academic vs personal 95
  active note-taking strategies 101–107 *see also* note-taking
  active reading strategies 98–101
  'bedraggled daisy diagram'

  search strategy 96–97
  date of publication 94
  different scales, at 95
  finding 95–98
  Google Scholar 96
  'grey literature' 94–95
  kinds of 93–95
  note-taking strategies 101–107 *see also* note-taking
  pacing yourself 99, 101
  primary and secondary sources 93–94
  publisher 94
  relevance of 98
  'scholarly source' 94, 95
  search strategies 96
  skim-reading 99
  targeted and time-efficient reading 98–101
  trustworthy secondary literature 94–95, 114
  untrustworthy secondary literature 94–95, 114
  worksheet 100

feather diagram 48–49
feedback to improve writing 89
'filler word' checklist 82–83
Fine, Gary Alan 99
'The active skim' 99
fishbone diagram 50–51

Google Scholar 96
'grading on the curve' 7
grammar 61, 75, 78
  active voice 67
  apostrophes 75
  ESL students 71, 72
  passive voice 62, 67–68
  preposition use 75–76
  reading academic English to improve 76
  sentences 62–64

high school writing 3, 6, 39

introduction 23, 24, 37
  background to problem 24–26
  context paragraph 25–26
  examples 24–25
  'funnel' 25–26
  'hooks' 24
  problem, statement of 24–25
  response to problem 24–25
  secret formula 24

worksheet 27
italics 85

language
    clarity 14–15, 61, 70
    ESL students 71–74
    hedging 68–69
    literary English 77
    neurodivergent students 72, 73
    online English 77–78
    'sentence skeletons' 56–57
    signposting 65–67, 70
    spoken English 76–77
    use of 'I' 62, 68 *see also* passive voice
LATCH theory of information 45
    Alphabetical 45
    Category 45
    Hierarchy 45
    Location 45
    Time 45
    worksheets 46, 47
learning management system (LMS) 11, 18
lecturers
    audience, as 7, 11–22
    comments, using 8–9, 10
    marking viewpoint 11–12
    requirements for essays 12–14
literary English 77
Luker, Kristin 96
    Salsa Dancing in the Social Sciences 96

marking *see* essay marking

narrative theory 57
neurodivergent students 72, 73
'norm-referenced' assessment 7
note-taking 101, 114
    connecting and synthesising 103, 106
    copying and pasting 111
    copying everything down 101–102
    Cornell method 108–110
    critiquing 106
    database tools 106
    digital strategies 106
    key terms and tags 107
    literature matrix, building 112–13
    note mapping 111–12
    note-taking templates 107–108
    paraphrasing 103
    plagiarism risks 102
    quoting 102–103
    reference managers 106–107
    summarising 103
    'synthesis' 102, 103
    worksheets 104–105, 110, 113
    writing and 107–108

online English 77–78

paragraphs *see also* body paragraphs
    length 15, 16, 28
passive voice 62, 67–68
Pauk, Walter 108

How to Study in College 108
phrasal verbs 77
plagiarism 11, 56, 102
planning 115, 128
    distractions, shutting out 122
    effective 'last-minute' writers 127–28
    fast writing 118, 119
    focus and 'flow state' 120–25
    multitasking 122
    'not list' 120, 121
    physical distractions 122–23
    Pomodoro Technique 124–25
    rough draft 118–20
    self-reflection 117
    sleep and rest, benefits 126–27
    thinking away from the desk 123–24
    time-box method 124–25
    time management 123
    time, tracking 115–17
    worksheets 116, 119, 121, 125
    writing to find plan 117–18
pleonasms 81
Pomodoro Technique 124–25
preposition use 75–76

quadrant diagram 54–55
quotations 85

Read, Siew Hean 75
    Academic Writing for International Students 75
reading strategies 98–101
    pacing yourself 99, 101
    prior knowledge, using 98
    questions using key words 98, 100
    searching-for-material phase and 98
    skim-reading 99
    worksheet 100
rubrics 7, 16
    attention to 16–18
    typical marking, example 17, 18

scientific theory 57
sentences
    confusing/unclear subject 63–64
    dependent clauses and 63
    grammar of 62–65, 70
    length 15, 64
    'skeletons' 56–57
sources, checking 80
spelling 75
spider diagram 52–53
spoken English 76–77
Sword, Helen 83
    The Writer's Diet 83

TESOL 74
theory, using 57
truth claims 40–43
    definition 40
    question, turning into 41
    statement of fact and, distinction 40
    worksheet 42

university essay
    argument aspect *see* argument
    body paragraphs *see* body paragraphs
    'boring', avoiding 19–21
    clear language 14
    conclusion *see* conclusion
    context, audience and discipline 18
    definition 6
    ease of reading benefits 14–15
    easy-to-read chunks 15–16
    essay question *see* essay questions
    focus 20
    good essays, examples of 61
    high risk suggestions 18–22
    introduction *see* introduction
    length 34
    marking 7–9 *see also* essay marking
    other writing, difference between 3, 6–7, 10
    'professional identity position' 20–21
    reading list 20
    reference list 23, 45
    review worksheet 33
    signposting content of 65–66
    small errors 16
    small requests by lecturers 16
    standing out from pack 18–22
    structure *see* argument; essay structure
    theory, use of 20
    what not to do 21

Wohl, Hannah 99
    'The active skim' 99
word count, reducing 80–81
    filler word checklist 82–83
    filler words, eliminating 81
    sentences, assessing 81
    sentences, deleting 81
    sentences, moving 81
workplace writing 6
writing
    academic 6–7, 10, 71–78 *see also* academic English
    audience for 6, 7, 11–22
    beyond essays, developing 129–30
    buddy, writing with 130
    clarity 15
    competitions 130
    editing skills 15 *see also* editing
    English, in 71–74
    high school 3, 6, 39
    low-stakes writing 129
    paragraph length 15
    public, for 129
    sentence length 15
    Wikipedia pages, editing 129–30
    workplace 6
Wurman, Richard Saul 45
    Information Anxiety 45

Zinsser, William 81–82

Lightning Source UK Ltd.
Milton Keynes UK
UKHW050821170321
380476UK00002B/18

9 781742 236803